To Elijah

The Angel's Metamorphosis

So nice to meet you
with all your light
gifts & interests ...

Hope we'll meet
again

Namaste
Karen .

The Angel's Metamorphosis

OR THE BOOK OF SHARAËLLE

Karen Benhamou Ruimy

QUARTET BOOKS

First published in England in 2010
by Quartet Books Limited
A member of the Namara Group
27 Goodge Street, London W1T 2LD

A catalogue record for this book
is available from the British Library

ISBN   978 0 7043 7188 0

Typeset by Antony Gray
Printed and bound in Great Britain by
T J International Ltd, Padstow, Cornwall

A Message from Sharaëlle

I am the angel who follows you, talks to you, loves you
I am here for you.
Nothing separates us
but your desire, your ignorance, your fear.
I love you and you know it not,
so leave now for the great voyage of love.
I will serve you as guide,
I will serve you as servant,
I will be there –
have no fear.
Know that this voyage is beautiful,
Know that it is your voyage, that of your own love
It is the journey that will lead you to find yourself again,
to love yourself.
It is your path
It is your voyage
Leave, you are the destination
You are afraid, above all of yourself
You have not lived what you are for thousands of years.

Preface

This book is a suggestion.

A suggestion for a path.

Towards love. Towards truth. Towards blossoming.
 Towards communication with the soul.

It is only a suggestion.

It is for you to be aware, to know, to try, to refuse,
 to be at ease with this book.

It is for you and you only to explore what is
 offered.

This is neither a model nor a theory, just an
 invitation to feel.

To feel through the grooves made by the tread of
 an angel.

To feel through inner dialogue, messages,
 sensations . . .

It is for you to choose.

Bon voyage.

Table of Contents

God

Let's talk about God.

There is no religious nor cult connotation with the entity I call God in the book.

God is representing the energy of creation, the universal force that has created us, that sustains us and that we belong to. We are, as living creatures, part of that entity.

Come With Me

I was lost.

I was happy among the larks.

I was bliss in the immensity of the void.

Serene. Alone.

☙

One needs to close one's eyes to behold . . . to see this realm of wonder where . . .

☙

In going back through the pages of this book I hear afresh the silence that enchants and softens me. I savour it. It enfolds me in a gossamer web of caring. It uplifts me from chaos. It bears me off into the gentle, into the sweet. It liberates me from harm and fear.

I had forgotten that happiness; I had forgotten the song of silence.

Why so? I forgot to remain silent. I forgot to stop.

Stop the lie. Stop forgetting.

So I forgot.

Running, talking, dealing: oh how I ran, ran, ran . . . I added a little more chaos to the chaos. We revisit chaos to learn. Learning how it flies, learning its voice. Understanding that it doesn't suit us, comprehending that it doesn't like us. Knowing that it commands us; it condemns us to falsehood, weeping, lashing out, abiding in fearfulness.

Yes, fear. We fear, so we speak out, we push. We push and we pollute. We pollute, and the smoke impedes our sight.

We need to close our eyes.

☙

Yes, I have alighted on this earth to denounce.

I have come to close your eyes. I have vowed to lift your vision in order to guide you far into the land of your dreams, the land of your childhood, the land of the divine. The divine that you are, the God you love. Indeed, at your deepest core you love your divine self. In your deepest awareness you love life.

Yet the love I speak of lies in the unfathomable deep. I am here to take you there.

Come with me.

A Broken Star

A short while ago, I discovered this ocean of love in which I lived, but which I had refused to perceive or to feel.

I am that ocean.

The ocean speaks to me. It has called to me for a long time. But I no longer believed in it; I had closed the shell and built a world inside this sealed shell.

I could not sense this immense, invading, obvious, drowning sea of love.

No, I had closed the sky over my head.

One day I knew fear in a storm.

I had been taught fear, the non-love, so I was struck by fear.

Gone was the unconditional love as I had known it,.

The celestial love that I carried at birth has been shattered.

I held it delicately in my fragile hands. I offered it without holding back. Certainly without holding back, for I was that love. I spoke, I chanted lyrics of love. I breathed the breath of love.

A star tumbled from the heavens.

The star was diffusing, giving, smiling, laughing, shining . . . until the day it was crushed into shards.

Its heart had been attacked by the lords of fear, the world order.

In this world love has no place. No: the world loves its limits, its conditions, its yes's and its no's. The world worships walls. The world loves to be quartered between four walls. No emptiness. No infinite space. Just limits: knowing where things start and where they end. No vastness, nothing incompressible, nothing impossible to control.

So, you, with your infinite, celestial love, could not return to the walled-in court.

Out of love for these sightless creatures, who were blinded by the shadow of the walls they put up, you followed them into the house.

Out of love, you left your nature in the entryway, between heaven and earth, where there is room for oceans.

Reduced, reduced, reduced, you played their game and you have forgotten. You, who are love.

You got caught up in the game.

New ideas for world order. You fed the world as it desired to be fed. Your energy was spent rebuilding walls, limits . . . Everyone was grateful to you. At last, an ounce of love.

✍

Yes, but all these efforts were expended at the sacrifice of my true nature, simply for a few drops of love.

I believed I would rediscover infinity.

I thought I could recall the joy of childhood.

As I built the other walls, I could not retrieve my serene, celestial joy, or my angel's laugh. No, with each wall constructed, I no longer felt even the comfort of 'security'.

I had to flee.

But where? Towards the infinite.

I no longer knew the way.

So piqued, I built more than ever, voraciously. To reach the summit, to see the sky.

For humans, the peak is to become rich; controlling, possessing, never lacking.

This bulimia of mundane success caused a terrible sickness. The spasms made my frame and spirit tremble.

My heart cried out but I did not hear it. I was too busy constructing this false dream.

I couldn't even find love within myself.

My castle stood empty.

My soul grieved. It was watching me; it despaired of being able to speak to me, to tell me it loved me.

I had lost my way.

Oh, to find again the gateway to this world, where I abandoned my true nature!

An Angel of Passage Among Us

Yes, I decided to take up the challenge of humanity. I resolved to become incarnate to help man to rediscover his divine essence, to rediscover love, to rediscover the profound meaning of life.

From above, I chose an ideal scenario to facilitate my apprenticeship into human life and my mission of elevation.

Of course, I came without any memory of this scenario so that I would better comprehend humanity in all its complexity.

I came in ignorance; therefore I had to recover the truth with help from above and from my own heart. The challenge was not limited to simply recovering my truth: I had to assume it and so become God's instrument in the nurture of humans.

As such I have lived a human existence – blindfolded, so to speak – where I too had to struggle to be loved, where I too had to believe in fear.

My soul has tolled the bell on this masquerade and thus violently disturbed the apparently happy course of my human life.

In the Land of the Invisible

I emptied my bag.

A richly adorned pouch, I turned it upside down. Everything tumbled out. I have nothing left. Materialism; the joy of materialism; the path of the ego, competition and the rest. No, none of that is left, and I feel so good. We feel so good when nothing is in front of us, no goal, no race . . .

Just being.

Being. Life passes. It streams by me. I honour it. I Am. That is all.

It is a strange state.

Living in nothingness. What lightness! What simplicity! What fullness! It is there – from this small nothingness, this grand void around us, this pure breath that engulfs us, this brightness of the morn that bathes us – that life rushes to salute me. Yes, it is there that creation springs. Out of the void streams the light. But why? How can the sublime be found in nothingness?

∞

The void is the reign of the invisible. The reign of the soul.

With the pouch emptied, radio turned off, ego assuaged, purity of heart and soul restored, we no longer hear, we no longer see. Anything.

At last we can hear the soul whisper words of love and truth in the hollows of our heart. We hear it say: 'Let us sing, let us dance, and let us leave for the invisible.' It invites us to guess, to grasp who we really are, that which was right beside this body; which, ever since birth, has been chasing material well-being, so-called opulence.

It is in silence that you will hear what the soul has to tell you. It loves you. It is you. It wants what is good for you, has done from

19

the beginning: nothing but good. It is only waiting for this moment to speak to you, to recover you, who have ignored it since your birth. Nevertheless, it is there, it speaks to you constantly, tirelessly, patiently, like a mother. You are its reason for being. But it knows most assuredly that you will hear it. It is there behind your noise, behind your illusions. It waits. Time does not count. Time does not exist in the land of the invisible.

Winds from Heaven

You are, you exist, you live, and suddenly you are no longer in harmony with what comes to you, or with the world. The events of your life assault you. You feel irritated without apparent reason, exasperated by the smallest happening.

You have lost control; above all, your smile. But where did your well-being and the joy of existence go?

You no longer master your serenity.

Know that heaven has spoken. It commanded your rattled mood and ordained an imperceptible, impalpable change in the air around us.

It is out of love that heaven has brought you this disruption. And yes, your soul has guided you. Your soul has taken you there where heaven has decided to blow the winds of change.

It is imperceptible but it is unbearable.

It's unbearable not for your soul, but for your ego.

Humans created the ego on the day they forgot to be God.

They forgot that they were the children of God, made up only of love; that their Father had sent them to spread love, the essence of creation.

They forgot: it is then that they took up fear.

They chose fear because unconditional love no longer surrounded them.

They disowned their divine nature and thus they lost their divine power of creation.

Fear of lack, of not being sustained, of losing freedom.

21

They believed in fear and so they fashioned themselves a realm of fear, separated from divine energy.

They experimented with a chain of fear, of non-love, of competition. They came to create an illusion of being outside of God and then outside of their soul.

And so the ego made its entry.

To survive, each being clothed himself in a new identity.

The soul could no longer respond, neither to fear nor to want. The soul, our presence at the throne of God, could not play the game. In this new world of illusion, humans had to find a substitute.

Each human fashioned a new state of being, a character that would face and survive these numerous fears.

Yes, the ego is a creation of fear.

Man separated himself from God and created the ego.

He detached himself from his soul and created a personality to fill the emptiness. He replaced his spiritual sense with his mental ability. He moved the centre of his existence to his reasoning mind, no longer in his heart.

Then he gave in to fear, he forgot this love which composed him, this love which rendered him divine.

It is true, you have forgotten to love. You have played the game of fear unwittingly. You have clung to the world of the ego. You deserted God.

You deserted yourselves. You abandoned your real essence. You stepped out of the divine flow. You built your own world and you live soulless. You are no longer in touch with your intuitions, your desires or the longings of your heart.

Then, to overcome all these fears, you made up a code of laws. The law of the strongest, the law of the most intelligent, the law of the richest . . .

A code of law and a code of being.

You became a cerebral sophisticate, disconnected from soul and love. You function according to these laws, according to the objectives of the ego's race.

To be more, and still more . . . Your heart no longer holds the key to the city.

∞

The ego is a tool of the mind. It will always take you far from your heart; from its murmur, its desires. The ego that you have created within yourself is a foreign body. It is the guardian of fear. You have let the world of fear influence you. The ego lodged itself in your mind. You created it to survive the fear and ever since, it has remained deep within you like a scarecrow.

∞

God your father watches you all the while.

You are utterly free.

Free to test this illusion, free to abide without love outside the divine flow. But your soul anticipates your awakening. It gives you signs, sends you messages. Symbols, encounters, accidents, hazards, injuries . . .

∞

At times heaven decides to shake up this world of illusion. Then the angels blow the winds of change in concert with your soul,. They send you a different energy, which engulfs you, confounding the ego you created. For a while this game, invented for your survival, will seem insupportable. You will feel an incomprehensible malaise, an urge to flee, a desire to stop everything.

Heaven's purpose is to stop you in your crazy egotistical race. You cannot do otherwise. Your arms and legs are paralysed. Your humour is out of control. Life becomes unbearable.

So you give up.

23

You find yourself without strength in the grip of a hurricane. You run for shelter.

※

The only shelter is found in your heart.

Your heart will deliver you from this nightmare. You need nothing other than to listen to it. At this point your guides – your guardian angels and your soul – will have accomplished their mission. They have made the foundation of your ego tremble. They brought you to this place of intense uncertainty where, perhaps, you can at last comprehend the illusion that surrounds you.

Doubt.

Finally, doubt. At last you see how far your steps have taken you from happiness and from love.

※

The ego is a box, in which you have locked up love; the love that you are and the love that the world expresses. It is a box that limits your nature, your freedom to exist. These are partitions of fear. They are mental lids. And you're in the middle, at the centre of a prison of illusions. An illusory prison. You will live there as if you had been created for it.

※

God is free. So are his children. God is love. So are his children. Fear is an illusion. Illusion cannot resist God. Fear cannot resist love.

※

To recover our nature, our origins. To rediscover God within.

Then you will be pure love.

The box will cease to exist, it will fade away.

※

We must gather these winds of energy, breathed forth upon our lands by the angels, in joy.

❧

Boxes do not resist. Unconsciously you are released from this prison. The prison detaches itself. You panic, for you have lost the habit of freedom.

❧

No, do not be afraid. Fear does not exist.

Celebrate the wind of growth; it is a wind of freedom, a wind of truth, a wind of love.

Awkward in the Light

Here I am, clumsy, a little silly, a bit ill-at-ease. I don't know where to put myself. I don't know where I am any more.

What I know is that I am. That's all. I am. I breathe. I love.

That sums up my state of mind today.

❦

I wanted to stop everything. I had suffered such a harried life. I had been stifled by the world of the ego. I screamed out. I had suffocated and one day . . . I left.

❦

I abandoned my laurels, my games, my politeness, my disguises, my stage props, my false desires and my challenges. Everything. Everything in the same bag, the bag of falsehood. The bag of the so-called. The bag of human games.

Humans only play at their humanity.

❦

To be born and allow oneself to play the game of death. The game of death and of fear – and primarily, of lacking.

We no longer come to earth to celebrate; we come now to struggle against deprivation, against the fear of deprivation, against the fear of fear . . .

Deprivation. Of what, pray tell? Deprivation of material and deprivation of time. So we stumble after things.

❦

I ran fast, perhaps too fast. I must have broken the clock. When I reached the mountain top, breathless, I wanted to clutch this dream, so long cherished and desired, with both hands. I wanted to hug it. And I found nothing there. Nothing to embrace. Nothing to cherish. Nothing at all. Still breathless, I opened my eyes and ears wider.

No, there was nothing. A terrible noise, yes. A clangour of chaos, a sound that was muted and unbearable at the same time.

I have seen others regain their breath at this very point and set out farther, higher, faster, convinced they will find it one day.

❧

My heart let go. It pinched itself so hard that I knew I had to stop.

Stop myself to listen at last.

That was how I spent several months removed from everything to find myself again: myself and my heart. We explained ourselves to each other. We spoke loudly. We fought. We ripped each other apart. We made up. We loved each other.

❧

For so long I have laboured so hard to build an ego, grander and grander, stronger and stronger, for the conquest of the world, the conquest of power.

❧

From now on I regard the world with a mother's love. A mother who watches her child tumble onto his face only to take his first steps. She knows that children must succeed by themselves to find their balance – alone and quickly free.

❧

Yes, when I ceased running, taking part in humanity's pursuit of the material, it all appeared so violently to me. Violently I understood the act humans put on when they leave childhood.

Violently I felt the ripping of this lie. I felt it in my flesh. I felt it in the innermost heart of mankind.

❧

Now I liberate my being and my life from this lie.

I to listen to my heart speak to me on waking.

I listen to my heart love or refuse throughout the entire day.

Here I am alone, my heart and I.

I have no more clever devices, I have no more so-called important activities; there is nothing left around me.

This time I have dug an empty space, a virgin space, pureness all around me, a blank page.

જ

A renaissance.

Yes, here I am new, to be reborn to humanity, free from lies.

Here I am ready to live life with the immense privilege of purity, of truth.

That's right, I feel awkward.

From now on, without lies, I have no visible protection.

Yes, but I am surrounded by truth, a formidable light.

Waking Up to the World

At dawn, at the glimmer of a new day,
    We belong to no one.
    We cling to nothing,
    We come from nowhere.

❧

We wake to the world each morning as a newborn does in the arms of his mother.

❧

He opens his eyes with naïve and authentic wonder.

❧

Each morning you relive this unknown second; it is a totally pure, virginal moment.

❧

Yesterday, when you went to sleep, you were someone with a history, with things, with reference points. You let yourself go, abandoned to sleep, everything left behind.

❧

In sleep, everything is flattened out, nothing matters, only you.
    You depart for a destination where no one, absolutely no one, knows the address or even its existence.

❧

It is a secret journey.
    It is an inviolable secret.
    You can be taken there only if you abandon yourself without restraint.

❧

When we sink into slumber, we have confidence, we love sleep, we have no fear of going there, we know what we will receive.

❧

Every morning God offers you this instant of purity, where you have no history, where everything is allowed.

❧

You rediscover your virgin state.

Your mind is completely free.

It is a second of eternity.

❧

So, each morning, seize this strand of eternity.

Love it and it will love you.

Speak to it and it will answer.

It will recount your mysteries, your hidden passions, your repressed yearnings.

It will let you discover love of the world, of birds, of flowers . . .

❧

It is an instant where desire is king. Nothing can keep you from loving, or from being yourself.

❧

Each morning, attempt to capture this divine purity that is in you. Try. Just for a second.

❧

Your eyes will open to the world. Don't let it come at you. Avoid that at least for a moment. Halt everything around you.

❧

And then you will experience a flash of immensity where you have neither limits nor fears. You can take leave to discover yourself.

Listen to Heaven's Voice

You blame your soul for not being there, for not smiling at you.

∞

It gives to you but you do not take what it gives you.

∞

It offers, but you close your eyes.

∞

You do not listen, so you formulate your desires from your ego, not in concert with your soul.

∞

So nothing can happen. The sound of its voice cannot reach your mind, the home of your ego where you create your blockages and your fears.

∞

Do not reproach heaven for silence if you decide to turn your back.

The Ego

We acquire ego from the eyes of others.

⚭

We open our eyes to the world and surprise looks of judgment, of scales, of weighing, of surveying, of counters, or jurors.

⚭

Your eyes were closed, there was nothing but love. Of love you breathed, in love you bathed. You felt the well-being; it had always been there. A white, infinite immensity.

⚭

You come to the world, you open your eyes. This is a picture in three dimensions: stopped, finished or to be finished.

Someone offers you a seat. Your mother's gaze requests beauty for you, your father's intelligence – or vice versa.

As you open your eyes, wishes that must be satisfied present themselves.

⚭

It is in that tiny instant that your ego is born.

⚭

You, alone in the world, will believe it. You must give them pleasure and honour their demands.

⚭

Your parents are also subjected to the same test. They too lost the freedom of being themselves, liberty in its primal essence. With liberty they also lost their lucidity. They allowed themselves to be taken in by the game of the ego, to the point of losing their memories. Even so, they wished the 'best' for you; unfortunately, it was the best in this game of illusion.

⚭

You open your eyes. They demand.

They will give you love in exchange.

It is only a morsel of love.

You were not accustomed to this.

Having had infinite love, you will now receive little pieces of love given out in reward for good deeds.

Know that these beings who welcome you have also lost their memory of infinite love. Humanity is organised according to the ego's kingdom and thus has dissuaded man from expressing his divine essence which is love.

⚘

Thus, to survive you will to have to conform to the rules of the world, play the game of bargaining love. You will gently abandon your light.

On arrival they give you laughter or sorrow, then fear along with their meagre crumbs of 'conditional' love – but you do not yet have words. By the time you have learned to speak, you will have forgotten who you were.

You will lose the notion of infinity, the infinity within you and around you.

⚘

The ego created at your birth will develop, activated every day to receive these tokens of love; the love that blemishes our precious humanity so deeply.

⚘

The veritable purpose of existence for every being is the quest for love, the divine essence.

⚘

In the world of the ego, this quest takes place outside of oneself, and quickly becomes a mad race for these little bits of love that we can harvest from someone else. The ego tries to make up for the emptiness left by the loss of infinite love.

⚘

In childhood, we turned away from the wondrous, inexhaustible source of love that is in all of us, out of fear of not being accepted.

And so we try to persuade ourselves that this source can be found outside ourselves, and thus we conform to this exterior world so that it may love us.

The Unveiling

Energy abounds.

Energy implodes in my body. It stirs deep into my gut. My throat constricts, I gasp for air.

Nausea.

∞

The ropes. Unravelling them, one by one; that is what I feel. Which ones? Always those that chain me to illusion. Always those which curb my freedom. The ropes no longer hold tight.

The energy is too strong. Like a raging ocean of crashing waves. A wind from the deep.

The ropes of childhood.

Childhood, when we took mere illusion for truth.

Childhood is the stronghold of our doubts, fears, humiliations, repressed desires and our lack of love.

∞

During this pure fragile period, we spin and knit our webs of protection against phantoms. Yes, phantoms and illusions.

The illusion of lacking love, the illusion of fear of the world, the illusion created by egocentric society, the illusion of power . . . All of this frightens the child. It distances him from his divine innocence, from his boundless love of self and the world.

Innocence is shattered. The child now shields himself.

These shields also belong to the world of illusion. And it is precisely these that will one day invade this being with a sense of limitation.

The limits to his freedom: the freedom to express himself; the freedom to love. Freedom. Love.

∞

This is what I feel. I have followed a path where I understood the illusion of the world. I tracked it. I cast it out of my life, out of my vision of the world. I cast it out more and more, unrelentingly. But today I must let go of the shields that I fabricated in childhood.

৯৵

Detachment from the past.

Detachment from old tricks, from those old arrangements that hold fear, from these masks.

৯৵

To abandon illusion means to recognise it, to cast it out and finally to relinquish the old tools that have enabled one to adapt to life's experiences.

৯৵

Take leave of the time of illusion.

Understand that we have journeyed to lands where the air is pure.

Thank your past.

Congratulate yourself for having understood.

Let illusion fly away on its own.

These ropes sever. My throat loosens up.

৯৵

All my life I tried to make myself loved. Please love me.

I didn't have it.

I didn't find it within myself.

So I invented many things: states, castles in the sky, all the heart-catchers.

I awaited the eyes of the world. I waited for it to stop at my crib side. I have charmed it ever since the day when love went astray, when my heart panicked. I have run across the world on this quest.

I have accumulated a lot.

৯৵

All this must leave me today. I must relinquish these things to the illusory world. All these cheap tricks.

৯৵

Just me. Me alone. Forgetting illusion and what I created to survive there.

⁂

Detachment is a painful ordeal.

Once a person understands that he must leave the world of illusion, all his masks will, at first subtly, then more and more forcefully, reveal themselves to him through uneasy experiences so that he can at last recognise and rid himself of them.

⁂

But the desire of purity is stronger than anything.

⁂

It is a sea wind, unstoppable.

The Trumpet Blew

I gathered my sages, my guides, and requested the immense privilege to come and take advantage from this Earthly paradise, to understand the human experience through incarnation.

That is how I came to be born here amongst you, to offer my celestial light.

This immense privilege temporarily deprived me of my memory.

✎

When one decides to live with humanity, one arrives veiled.

Veiled to better experience human reality and the truth of matter. Without memory of identity or mission, you give yourself up to the game.

You are your mother's baby. The world welcomes you with its laws, its usages, its fears and its illusions. When your memory is still strong and present you do not possess a voice. After you learn the language, the world has already assigned you your role and its scene and your recall is blurred.

✎

So you play. Everyone plays. You, too, buy into it.

We play to elude fear.

The perfection of this game is disturbed by flashes of memory.

They come to you in an unsuspected, unforeseeable manner.

You recite your lines and suddenly there is a glitch, a memory hiccup.

✎

That's right, smack in the middle of your studious human life, your soul comes to wake you up.

It comes to disturb you on stage.

You had gotten used to the world of matter, of limitation. You had tamed that savage beast called fear.

There your soul comes and whispers in your ear:

Stop, we have come to denounce the hoax.

∞

We played in order to understand the rules and mechanisms of the human world.

It is time to discard the masks.

∞

Do not believe that my soul arrived like a letter delivered by mail. Not at all! It was manifested through the most subtle of heavenly means.

Stages of the soul.

Yes, I have experienced strange, inexplicable sensations, impossible to rationalise by reason or potion.

Simply a slightly different state of being. It is bizarre. Simply different. My body was no longer sufficient.

My heart got carried away.

I was gripped by impatience. With what, tell me?

This was the mystery of my human life.

∞

From one state of soul to the next, I listened to the irrational, since no remedy or rational explanation could get to the bottom of this mystery.

I opened the door to the mystery.

After a fear, a mistrust borrowed from humans, I welcomed it into my arms. It prowled through every act of my human endeavour.

First, we pierced the ceiling of the unconscious with Freud.

∞

This divine mystery that swept me away in enthusiasm and worry was not always unveiled through analysis.

Freud shed light on our human role on earth.

I thank him for this.

But my soul was sending me indecipherable signals through human science and through magic.

❧

The magic of life. The rain stops, the sun welcomes you when you arrive. Doors open along the way. The doors close, without reason or explanation.

I knew profoundly. Magic had always existed here, for me and for everybody. Nothing could persuade me otherwise.

❧

So I searched for the original breath of magic.

I asked.

Yes, I cried into the void, to God or to no one, waiting for nothing in particular.

❧

I asked the cosmos.

Since the day I asked, I have received the profound yet silent message that my life goes on here below and there above, there and here, without boundaries. I have grown into that certitude.

They let me grope about blindfolded in this state of transformation, of openness to another reality.

They let this message bring me to the lands of doubt and those of certainty, to the corners of misery and the halls of ecstasy.

Ecstasy to feel the light. Ecstasy to feel in tune. With what?

Just be in harmony, without any reason.

Living confidently, although blindfolded, without guarantees or promises. Hoping without assurance. It was this or nothing.

Once we have recognised the mystery, we can no longer live without trying to create light.

❧

One beautiful spring day a trumpet blew.

My friend Gabriel. He came disguised as a fairy. For a while he strode by my side, demeanour unremarkable, trumpet invisible, sound inaudible.

Gabriel's trumpet sounded in my being and love flooded me.

I was given back the confidence that I had so generously given heaven.

Gabriel, my own soul, and others helped me unveil the truth, layer by layer.

My eyes began to see again.

My heart once more felt the freedom of being. The engineering was perfection. So was the orchestration.

An Angel Tests Illusion

What is this recurring despair? It is so unbearable when this malaise resurfaces.

I stumble into dissatisfaction, into quicksand. It is difficult to climb out. I am hot. I am sweaty. My skin sticks to me. My body feels heavy, so heavy. My limbs are swollen. I am losing my lightness, my ability to fly, my freedom.

Yes, I understand. I knew it already. I know.

✧

Here is an angel, come to see the world of the ego.

She wished to taste it. She hardly got her feet wet. She let herself be pulled in by the force of illusion.

She wants to return, because she does not feel well. But her wings have become stuck in matter.

It is so painful, so very difficult to get back. In reality, she has to find her own truth again, the true awareness of her being.

In coming here, she has lowered her level of consciousness in order to participate in this illusion, this game humans play at being away from God, outside their own divinity.

It is a quicksand, where purity sinks. It is impossible to survive without protection, without knowing how to manoeuvre within it.

The angel herself does not know how. She must live the illusion without forgetting that it is illusion.

✧

Yes, that's it, I came in a human body.

I came to live without my wings.

It was a new challenge.

My mission is to denounce illusion, to free humanity from the bog.

I chose to incarnate in a body in order to learn, to understand this quicksand, to understand how to get out . . .

It is a difficult route.

It is a path through trial.

I won't be able to save anything if I don't demonstrate for myself that road to freedom. And who would be inclined to follow me?

Yes, at this moment I suffer from the falsehood that I myself created and in which I live.

I let myself go.

I know. I knew. It's strange, there are things we know and yet . . .

To forget the truth is to enter into the world of illusion and the ego and to lose oneself in the game.

It is then that something clicks.

Confusion enters you. Your soul is unhappy, because you have decided to play the game and believe in it.

I went off to frolic from the start, or almost.

I was born with a veil over my eyes.

I came not knowing.

Little by little, I awakened from this lie.

Calls from heaven, messages from my soul: everything led me into the malaise of ignorance and of doubt.

Yes, I was living this game but I knew that the rules were rigged.

I had to throw myself into the search for truth.

My spirit went back to the light.

I saw. I understood that mankind lived in a world of illusion, in the kingdom of the ego.

∞

Then I went to live in the sky with my guides and my soul, but my body was still drenched with illusion.

∞

Yes, me too, I participated in this world, I created from matter, I built a theatre, I donned roles to fit my persona.

Then one day I unveiled this game and I rediscovered my true nature. I needed to stop the game in order to return to love and joy.

∞

This illusion, these roles, this theatre: we invent them to live the experience of humanity, of emotions. It is an apprenticeship.

∞

We create the illusions to protect ourselves from the aggression of the world and to draw love towards us.

They are proof that we need love.

But love is in us.

The illusion is the road sign that we have lost the use of our love, for ourselves and for others.

∞

Each illusion is created to mask a lack of love. It is also a sign.

Search it out.

You will discover that you lack love and you will know the reasons. Then you can heal yourself, give yourself that which you lack – love.

A World of Love

Being human really is less enjoyable for me. You are born human and then, all of a sudden, your gifts are revealed to you, you can no longer play the game, the truth looms before you, light illuminates, and you know.

෧

You hear different people's thoughts. Their eyes speak to you, tell you where they have come from, what they have known, what they are longing to live . . . all these secrets that your mind does not dare to confess. These beings tell you something, and you hear their innermost soul tell you the opposite.

You look up: someone is clothed in the costume of our times and then suddenly a totally different image superimposes itself on this being – a monk, a child, a repenting tyrant . . . but always the same eyes. He tells you of his sorrows, of his yearnings. All the while his soul cries out something else.

෧

It is strange, you know, dear humans, to hear you entirely.

෧

Yes, I came from another world.

A world where one is light and love.

Our bodies are fluid. Our contours are hardly discernable. The white light that streams from us is sweetly dazzling.

It is an aura, a mist that immediately encircles.

It is a cloud of love. Only love. Pure and simple. Tender love. Strong love.

It is a world where love is obvious.

It is the fluid that we are made of, that which surrounds us.

It is what constitutes our unique power, our unique force.

Unique but powerful.

Believe it, my loved ones, it is a breath that lifts up mountains, a fluid that builds temples, it is a creative thought.

❧

Yes, it is the gift of God.

You are made of love only.

Your reason for being is love.

You are saturated with the divine force.

You are a messenger, or a worker of God.

You are only a part of Him.

Your heart, soul and personality are merged in one, in Him, your Creator.

Your desires reach from the heart of God, so that each stands as a command in the cosmos.

All desire calls forth its manifestation.

❧

It is a world that surrounds you, dear humans.

The beings from beyond love you tenderly.

They look after you but you do not see it.

They speak to you; they explain the threads of wisdom and joy. They are there, each moment of your life.

Of course they are invisible to your eyes but your soul lives near them. They so want to help you. They would love to help you, that is their mission, but you forgot them when you arrived here.

Then you forgot that they were right beside you, on the other side of the veil.

The veil that prevents you from perceiving them is the same one that hides you from your soul, from God.

Behind this veil all is love. Behind this veil . . .

❧

Blow, blow.

Tell us your true desires.

Tell us about you, the real you.

You, sublime beings.

God created you, entirely of love.

But, you had the courage to come to Earth and experience forgetting.

How brave you are. I admire you, Loved Ones.

Now, reveal yourselves to me.

If the veil is imperceptible, speak to me from the depths of your heart. Murmur it, write it. I hear it because my soul surrounds you.

Your thoughts resonate in me. You suffer, you laugh, you pray . . . I hear it, we hear it in our realm.

Do not be afraid. Come to confide in us.

∞

Open the sky.

Talk and hear. Listen to the silence. I promise you, you will hear a murmur.

It is a word of love.

It will guide you toward the light.

We are there day and night, eternally.

This is our role in the world of love.

We are there in service to God.

He has bestowed on us the immense privilege of sacrificing us to love.

It is an oath taken before Him, to be in His service completely. I tell you that we derive the most sublime ecstasy in the Universe from it. I know that the word sacrifice is disturbing to you, dear humans.

Yes, we are there omnipresent, without the limits of time and space. Such is our nature.

Such is your true nature, that of your soul.

Life Without Joy

The power of joy is astounding.

This morning, my waking was muted.

My body surfaced from slumber but my spirit remained in a place I couldn't quite define. I was awake but certainly not awakened. I went back to sleep. No, I have not found the answer to this malaise there.

❧

It is a state where your physical substance, your mortal body, is ready to function. Yes, it is a state of functioning but not of existence.

I was alert but life had no flavour. So I got up to dispense with the day mechanically. That was all that was left to me.

No inclinations. No joy. Nothing jolted me into emotion.

Of course I was worried. I knew that the link to my soul had been cut clean.

My soul awaited me. It had blocked my joy of living in order to express it to me.

❧

To live without one's soul, without listening to that inner self that offers us joy, is to function mechanically.

In this state, we begin to reason, to plough through the world, to organise, without contact with the true joy of the heart. We get wrapped up in the rules of the world.

❧

Once we are disconnected from joy, it is hard to return to it. In this state, we try to understand, to explain away the malaise; we seek out the many solutions the world offers us. The more we try, the further away we get.

When you feel dull and sad, without desire, taste or passion, stop in your tracks. Know that your heart has stopped to speak with you, to forewarn you that you are on a path that does not please it.

∞

Your heart is the correspondent of your soul, of God. It knows. It knows the nature of your essence; it is part of it.

It knows the grooves of joy. It knows what your gifts and your passions are.

So go back to it, and let it express the reasons for its muteness. Let it untie the knot of your worries and blockages.

A Well of Love

I feel like an enormous well of words, ready to explode, but I have nothing to say.

Are they really words, are they really messages, are they really things to say? Perhaps I have only my loving regard to bestow.

❧

Indeed, it is a matter of love.

I have a desire to tell the world that I finally know the purest love.

I love this person at the core of me.

I love her without constraint, without limits. Finally I love her. Yes, finally.

❧

I fled the world, I shut my door and I searched.

I searched for why this bit of discontentment struck at my heart, my spirit.

Dissatisfied, anguished. Always becoming.

Marvels, riches, trophies accumulated around me but nothing would do. There was always this agonising, unexplained wound.

I closed the door. Then I looked around.

❧

I unveiled. I discovered. I gave the world back its treasures.

My house was empty. Empty except for me. And there, alone with myself, I began to comprehend.

Once again I honoured my true joys, I celebrated myself, I honoured the marvel that God had created.

I discovered just one thing, a being made of love.

The rest didn't belong to me.

❧

I loved.

There. The more I discovered the essence that enfolded me, the more I purged myself of the substance fabricated by our civilisation.

No more substance, I was becoming emptier and emptier.

৵

This emptiness that we discover is always terrifying.

৵

We have spent our lives tossing about, to pad out emptiness. We never learn to live in the emptiness.

This void is simply each being's immense capacity to create and convey love.

Once we understand that, we want only one thing, to empty ourselves further. Again, again . . . to be nothing but this bubble of love that God sends at birth.

৵

So today, I love.

I exist only for that.

I walk in the street and encounter all these beings, I yearn to cry out their love to them, I yearn to show them the way.

It is a path that will lead you to you, to your sublime being of love.

The Gift of Truth

I have wiped away so much.

No more masks, no more lies.

What is left?

The passage of time. Solitude. Me. And love.

Me, life and love. That's all.

I came back to the departure point. I came back to the contract that God had always given me.

Oddly enough, I have the urge to write about what this force is that suddenly comes upon us on our journey.

One day, you decided to stop the comedy of life, feeling that something was amiss in this world. So much fakery, so many causes of heartache, so many appalling events. You endured it for a long time; you played the game endlessly, believing you were able to explain things away.

But no, the more you play, the more you suffer, the more the world appears unreal and revolting. Then one day you decide to get up from the table.

You leave it without markers, without protection, or predictions. You leave on the spur of the moment. It was too much.

So, like a scatterbrained child, you leave without warning, you forget the way to school and you dive into adventure, lured by the unknown.

You are profoundly aware that something awaits you. You know that there, you will find a fragment of truth, so you go.

It's a quest.

I go to hunt the truth.

Nothing resists any more, not even you.

You: this personality that you have forged day after day with the conviction of a warrior.

You walk alone with nature, sweeping away your attitudes and judgments. They appear vain now, they fade away.

It is a naked road.

Yes, you will be cold, you will be frightened, you will wish to have your clothes back from time to time – for you were used to wearing them as an armour against the menace of this world.

୧

Above all, continue, this is a test of faith.

୧

Truth is a gift one must offer oneself.

Truth does not offer itself like a costume or a role.

Truth is a state of being.

One must desire it, with the irresistible urge to become a true being once again; pure, cleansed of the lies of the world.

One day you open your eyes to the world and you understand that you have given yourself the most precious gift in the world.

You breathe the pure air of this world. Yes, the air is pure once you have recovered your innocence.

As pristine as on the day of your birth. Then you remember the question that loomed in your head: *why did I come?*

୧

You came to love.

To love.

God gave you life to love.

Loving is the supreme power. God is love. God acts through love, to spread Himself, to spread love. Thus God created us. In His image. Yes, He created beings of love with the only material with which He is comprised, love.

You came to spread it, you also, on this earth, in this world of matter. But you let yourself fall under the spell of this matter.

53

In this world, we certainly love, but in fragments, and under certain conditions.

You arrived with your immensity of love.

Little by little, you packaged it in small boxes, you weighed it out . . . you forgot your mission. You endeavoured to squeeze infinity into your little containers. That is why you are so miserable in your human role.

So open these boxes, forget your obligations and recall your nature.

God has lent you life with this condition, the infinite.

Yes, it is difficult to accept this gift.

The Act of Being Different

In recent days I have had moments of unreasoning anger. Suddenly, a violent wave of anger arises inside you and nothing prepares you for it. That has been my experience. I sought to understand it. It was after several days in this state, difficult both to control and to admit to, that tears of helplessness opened the way for comprehension.

∞

I had buried this anger that was now resurfacing a few years ago. It is a very strong emotion caused by a painful incident. An episode where I decided to abandon a social situation that was comfortable and enviable, against all expectation.

This act unleashed angry reactions around and against me. I had fractured the crystal bubble in which 'honour', 'dignity', and 'ambition' were preserved.

∞

My decision to quit the world of usages and custom undermined the model then in place.

∞

This model no longer suited me: neither me nor my stifled heart.

∞

So I took off. No one believed it, because I was so disciplined.

But despite no one believing it, I left.

Some judged, while others reacted with a certain vehemence.

∞

And I was left alone to face the whole of this honourable world, feeling weak in spite of my uncompromising decision.

I knew I had to leave, for I could no longer breathe, but I was afraid.

I did not know the road ahead of me.

I found myself without protection for the first time in my life.

I had the courage to leave but on the inside, I was afraid.

What would happen to me without this system that surrounded and pampered me?

Gripped in this fearful energy, I let myself listen to their fury, and so I came to understand that their world really was no longer a match for me.

I was the target of anger and I suffered, but I did not respond because I did not know what the future held; because I did not have total confidence in my future.

Thus, I was subjected to anger without expressing my own.

I suffered deeply from this violent and sudden rejection, where in the blink of an eye I tumbled from the 'queen's' pedestal to the status of 'outcast' simply for behaving differently.

This difference was my survival.

This difference showed me the road to freedom but I had to suffer the inevitable distress that goes along with a system based on illusion.

This was the sufferance of someone who abandoned everything, or at least the illusion of everything, in order to respect her difference, her truth.

An absolute act of honouring oneself.

This absolute stings, for it manifests in you before reaching true maturity.

My difference was present and very strong within me, but I had not entirely assimilated it into my consciousness.

So I battled with blurred eyes.

The only thing I felt profoundly was the need to fight, to depart.

So I did but I gave them my weakness, my immaturity, and in return I received their scorn.

❧

I had honoured my heart by my leaving, but I dishonoured it by my fear of the morrow, in accepting the judgment and the anger of others.

Then I left in the sufferance of being disowned, and even more, misunderstood.

I swallowed all that, all my resentment toward those who no longer respected me in my choice. I swallowed all my tears. I held it all in so as not to weaken or play their angry game. I wanted to show false indifference, so I lied, to answer the call of my soul.

❧

Answer the call of the soul without reason.

❧

Today this anger resurges like an old ghost.

Yes, I am now strong enough to face this truth, to understand this anger, this circumstance of non-love I went through.

I hold enough love, compassion and lucidity for all those who repudiated me in the name of their sacred belief of the world's dominion.

I see the illusion in which they live, and which they take to be the unique truth. I see how they themselves lack understanding and love.

❧

Where I am now, I no longer judge them.

Now this repressed memory may resurface, because I can embrace it now with the eyes of compassion. For them and for me.

❧

Thus my soul orchestrated the perfect scenario for these reunions. It was a question of recognising this repressed part of me that was filled with pain, suffering and anger.

57

For the first few days, I felt a strange and inexplicable resurgence of anger. Then, through extraordinary coincidence, I saw the actors of this old period again; I had to start to understand everything, and, above all, to reconnect our energies to begin the purification of my emotions.

Finally, again by chance, I found myself at the screening of a movie. From beginning to end I wept through this endearing film. Evidently, I wanted to understand. It was the story of a young girl who had 'dishonoured' her family and her background of strong and uncompromising ancestral custom through love.

Merciful God, something clicked!

I went home and this time I wept over my own story. I eased my suffering. I have laughed a lot about the scenario my soul set up to reactivate my memory.

Then I felt at peace, having refound this repressed part of myself, able at last to identify this inexplicable anger

I understood.

I loved.

I honoured my soul.

The Ego is Mischievous

The ego is sometimes stronger than you.

❧

You have decided to chase it away from you.

You have detected it.

Crudely, then mischievously, it installed itself inside you.

Its presence became more and more subtle.

It lodged behind your eyes, behind your spirit, always gaining in cunning on its way to elevation. It is a hunt.

You have decided to liberate yourself from the ego of the world, which taught you the rules of good and the less good from birth; the rules of the best, the laws of comparison, of competition, of judgment . . . of non-love.

❧

Sometimes, in the effort to combat this mischievous imposter, you exhaust yourself, your body runs out of steam, your eyes pucker. It is a fatigue without reason. It is a profound weariness, which resists everything.

❧

It is a blockage. It is a kind of nausea. It is very strong.

Nausea keeps me from living, from celebrating joy.

Actually, nausea is nothing; it is imperceptible to the eye and yet it is a state which prevents me from awakening in joy, from laughing, from smiling. Moment by moment, life becomes a burden.

❧

Since the day that I re-encountered my old companions, this nausea has not left me.

A cue from my soul.

❧

There is a dull discord inside me.

True enough, I do not understand.

What helplessness, to suffer without knowing the cause! I know only that my soul is sending me a message.

A message that is not understood.

∞

The nausea installed within me, my life is spent wandering. I flit from thing to thing, person to person, activity to activity.

I search.

∞

I have lost the taste for pleasure.

I have lost my joy.

So here I am, on a quest.

Not to read, nor to write. Running, shouting, singing . . . nothing will do.

∞

Tears.

When joy no longer sweeps through you, you start by wandering, before confusion and, finally, tears fill your eyes. Too much grief. It is a tempest. You wish for a strong destructive storm, to destroy this heavy and oppressive atmosphere that prevents you from flying away.

∞

Tears, revelations. Finally, your heart speaks.

∞

That party was my opportunity to re-encounter all the people I spent time with before I quit the social circle. They were the architects of my ego. They are part of the world that I was determined to drop. They were intolerant at the summit of the world ego; succeed or be worthless.

∞

From where I am today, I see them with clarity acquired day by day, which freed me from the yoke of ego and social rules. I see them. I also see myself.

I see the game I played with them.

I present myself to them, observing their expectations, which I created and left in their hands a few years back. These expectations are still there. They are the result of our mutual creation, that of our egos.

❦

Some people set up new rules for success, others accomplish them, and so on.

And in the process everyone is mirror to everyone else.

Only those who managed to fulfil the goals of competition were loved.

❦

A true athletes' track. Sharpened egos lie in wait for their competition. The goal is always to do better, specifically better than the others.

❦

To create a system of values. Money, beauty . . .

❦

To set the limit always higher.

To obtain their love, in order not to lose this energy made of admiration or of jealousy that I received from these egos, I always placed the limit a bit higher. Then I defied them, and I left to conquer this never-attained summit anew. Companions in ego. A game of spirals.

❦

This is a competitive game, a game based on judgment and on fear of not succeeding.

❦

A game where you lose yourself in fear.

❦

Yes, I left without screaming 'beware'.

❦

I quit the game table. Not them. They continue to carry out their task.

And me? Where did I go?

⚭

I fled that life because I did not dare to tell them the truth. Like a coward I departed to find myself, to detach myself from that ego that suffocated me. I knew I was strong enough to leave, but also fragile to show myself. I headed for the unknown without knowing what awaited me.

⚭

At that instant I still harboured fear of the unknown. I knew that if I stood before them at this moment I would weaken and *that* I did not want.

⚭

I was leaving on a grand voyage and I wished my ship to be strong. I knew the mischief of the ego well; I had built it and thus foresaw their insidious and destructive machinations, undertaken for the sole, simple purpose to drag me back into the game. The game is more exciting when the players are numerous and competitive.

⚭

Today I present myself to them squarely; they interrogate me right away on the criteria they themselves endeavour to fulfil.

⚭

But they get nothing. Nothingness. Unconditional love.

Someone who has let go of her laurels. Their egos evidently attribute this to defeat. She has let go, those were her limits.

Yes, surely, my life had become intolerable.

I had lost my taste for living.

I had to stop this infernal mechanism which I had collaborated to create and in which I participated.

To stop. That is all.

To stop the manipulation of the world ego; to cease to amplify it, refine it, bedevil it in order to become the master, in order to own the power. To become free again.

62

Man Does Not Love Himself

Man does not love himself.
   Man does not listen to himself.
   Man does not know himself.
   He underestimates himself.
   He loves nothing but the trickeries of society.
   He loves himself through others.
   Man does not hear his heart, he barely tries . . .
   He ignores this marvel that he holds in his hands.
   Then he searches everywhere for a goal of his existence . . .
   But it is in him that everything waits to be discovered . . .

The Game of Perfection

To be absolutely perfect, absolutely, for always . . .

A beautiful body, a brilliant mind, an emotional equilibrium, a perfect heart that is neither too big nor too small . . .

Well turned out, educated, successful, an impressive presence . . .

The list is long, the list never stops; it fills a whole life, indeed several.

Filling, filling, filling.

Seducing, seducing, seducing.

∽

Where are we? In a game.

A game where the actor never ceases to play until his costume cracks. He himself must never crack.

The costume cracks.

It is at this point that the great disillusionment begins. Like a game of dominos, life unveils itself before you, game after game, lie after lie.

You were the king of lies.

∽

Today you can no longer play, your costume is cracked.

What to do? Where to go? What is there behind the scene?

You are afraid because no one or almost no one lives there. In any case, no one really dares to speak of it.

A costume cracks, we replace it.

But no, it is impossible; you know that; you can no longer play this game of perfection.

∽

Yes, I too can be without morality, I can be without courage, I can be without knowledge . . .

Yes, I am also terribly imperfect in the eyes of humanity. Believe me. I have lied to you about myself. I am not the extremely solid being that I prefabricated in my youth and education.

I am not the one who claims perfection and nothing but.

I am nothing other than a simple woman.

❧

I played. Forgive me. I fooled you. I did it to please you. So that you would love me. I was too fearful of being dismissed as a 'villain' or an 'idiot' or . . .

❧

Heaven sent me to speak the truth.

I only am here for that, to tell you that you are the children of God, that you are beings of light and that the time has come to return to the light.

❧

It is time to jump out of the illusion that you have created, which you call 'humanity'.

It is time to become human once more and to give back your costume.

Dare.

Deep within you, you dream of it, you have awaited this moment for so long, to cease the struggle.

❧

Yes, you have warred against yourself for so long.

You have fought your true nature as a child of God, made of love and of light.

You fight.

You have become the warrior of illusion.

❧

But where are you, who are you behind this shield?

❧

Feel.

Search well.

Are you sure that you want to battle? To wish always, always to reinforce your ego? To want to win at any price?

❧

Are you absolutely certain that you were not made for love?

❧

Sense it. Feel it out.

Silence your combat.

Listen to your heart.

❧

Still want to act?

No, I know it; I see it in your eyes, disillusioned by the meaning of life.

You stage this play because you know nothing else.

I am here to tell you that.

I have lived this act to understand it better, to better unveil it.

Joy Has Left Me

Joy has left me.

Since then, I have descended into gloom, far from myself. I can't find myself again. It is a state of absence.

A survival. Each moment carries then only problematic choices.

❧

Once joy leaves, simplicity goes too.

Nothing is simple any more. Always the need to choose laboriously in order to divine where to find well-being, or at least its path.

❧

Joy is simple. The path to it is simple.

❧

But when we lose joy, we lose ourselves in places that do not belong to us, in models, duties, obligations, on so-called roads to success.

❧

I know the way is simple but I have lost the sense of it, I no longer know where my heart beats. I no longer know how to silence the noises that invade my mind. Anxious, fearful noises. Noises that get tangled up. Never in harmony, nor in rhythm.

❧

I no longer hear the melody of my heart.

Oh, to calm this tyrannical din, this confusion.

Confusion is a noisy anarchy that has overthrown the power of the heart.

❧

To create silence.

To quiet the chaos.

To become simple again.

To rediscover cohesion.

To strike out anew on the path of the heart . . .

To listen again to its murmurs. To yield again to the suaveness of its expression. To grant its desires. To love self . . .

Joy has returned.

The Energy of Joy

You need 'concrete advice'. But you have no needs. The only pathway towards light and well-being is to be yourself.

To be more precisely, to be to the utmost, to be ceaselessly, to be everywhere.

❧

To be is to love life.

To be is to celebrate life in each moment that goes by.

The road of existence is travelled by listening to you and your soul.

❧

At each moment, ask yourself if you celebrate the life which passes through you.

❧

To celebrate life simply means feeling joy.

So, build yourself an altar, the Altar of Joy.

Each morning wake yourself and ask your soul what day this is and what joy awaits.

❧

Wake from your celestial journey and leave your feats on the Altar of Joy.

Each day brings you infinite gifts of joy. It is up to you to receive them, to live them. It is there that you will find God.

It is in the radiance of joy that you will feel the thrill of God, the supreme smile of that which has given you life, of that which you became in receiving life.

❧

Before the Altar of Joy, drop all your projects, simply be. You are.

❧

Then the divine flow will sweep you up. You will let yourself drift, without expectations, smoothly, without habits.

❧

It is in this sublime unknown that your heart will speak to you, guide you along the paths of well-being, joy and ecstasy.

❧

If by accident you should escape from ecstasy, if the fogginess overtakes you, then stop everything.

Rest a moment. Close up your house. Close down your body. Call the light.

Feel the light sweep through you from your crown to the tip of your toes.

Let the light pass from the sky to the earth through you, as a conductor.

❧

Breathe deeply.

Inhale God, again, and again.

Feel God entering every corner of your body. Move your hand, look at it. God has returned. Your hand moves with divine energy.

Now you have saturated your body with energy and light. You have stilled your mind and the emotions that tugged at you at the gaming table.

Finally, appeased, you can retrieve the true question or the single command in the service of God: 'Engage that which renders me happy, joyful, peaceful, loving, beautiful and luminous.

Where is my joy?'

❧

Joy is a perfect accord between life and soul.

❧

When we find ourselves shrouded in fog, we are like the pianist who has lost the chord in the middle of his notes. Suddenly the symphony shatters.

❧

We must abide in harmony between life and soul, that of the dance between them.

∞

Go now and live in the world, in your joy. Observe the games of humans.

At each moment, choose the way of the heart.

Stride toward realisation without fear or worry.

Choose roads where doors open before you.

∞

In joy, you will always be preceded by angels.

They will deal with everything. You will recognise them again by this sign. They will signal you with their magic gestures. They will clear the way before you, they will remove all obstacles. They are at your service. In the fog they cannot aid you, divine energy cannot pass; your receptor is obstructed by fears and by illusion.

∞

Your life unfolds as on a magic carpet. It glides forth. Your only clue to walk on it is joy. On the carpet one is transported by wings.

∞

Do not lose the magic.

Let joy and the angels lead the way in all domains as everything is part of your path, even the most minor tasks, where your eyes see no interest.

Welcome each experience as a new apprenticeship of life and of joy.

∞

Each thing, each event given you is the realisation of your own wishes. Understand their messages.

Even at its 'vilest' and most 'materialistic', choose well-being, reach for the choice of the heart, the angels will take charge of the rest. Don't turn your back on your heart; it knows what is good for you and for others, even though reason makes you feel guilty.

Always favour the joy of your heart; you will see that you render the entire world joyous.

71

Be joyous, and your eyes will illuminate the world around you, it is the most beautiful gift you can offer it.

Be joyous, and you will give them the way of light. Be joyous and you will show them joy. One day, they will follow you.

❧

Joy cannot be built. Joy cannot be predicted.

❧

Humans have always laboured in order to obtain joy, to deserve it.

❧

Joy is lived day to day, in the moment. Joy drinks of itself without waiting. It does not prepare itself. It is. It gushes out. Joy is a state of being. It is ephemeral. We must cultivate our yearning, our desire to be joyful, just as we breathe oxygen, as we nourish our bodies . . .

❧

Here is the recipe. Simply choose the way of joy.

❧

Joy will then weave an aura of luminosity and energy around your being.

❧

Joy is food for the soul.

To be joyous brings formidable energies. Joy floods the soul with celestial energies. This spiritual energy then will spread itself to the four bodies: spiritual, emotional, mental and physical. Besides that, energy will flow into every intention.

❧

Joy is indeed the purveyor of energy into each being. It works on the being itself and on all its accomplishments.

❧

The being who lives in the divine flow formulates his desires and intentions in spiritual purity,. These desires float in the atmosphere, awaiting the energy impulses that will bring them into being.

❧

In being joyous, we set free torrents of celestial energy, which will rush in to lodge in these bodies in formation which are our intentions.

Freedom of the Heart

It is clear that a long time ago I buried undesired aggressiveness within myself. Today it resurfaces when someone tries to shield my liberty, my lightness.

؆

I had a strict upbringing, without much choice or freedom to express, create or evolve. A real social and cultural dictatorship of studies, religion, social behaviour, male-female distinctions, taboos . . .

؆

Today I feel strong inner violence when someone attempts to throttle my liberty, my spiritual truth.

؆

My companion suggests practical responsibilities that do not please me and which feel very foreign to me. I then feel guilty for not participating in collective activities.

Hence, out of guilt, I fling myself into it. I accept the responsibility.

But then this disrespect for my desires inevitably leads me to internal anger. My companion multiples his demands. My anger grows and accumulates. And I feel drowned in outlandish concerns and pollutants.

Little by little, I suffocate.

Anger creates in me a negative energy field which spreads out anew every time that these subjects come up again. This negative energy increases to the point of explosion.

؆

It is obvious that the more I act against the pull of my heart, the less easily matters work out.

My companion is, without doubt, ideally placed to reawaken those pockets of non-light, of disrespect for myself. Unconsciously, he triggers these angers so that I can understand and heal myself.

∾

In this difficult game, he represents the human world in three dimensions. This world would have me behave according to its rules, for the so-called 'good of the world'. And I, who have no wish to comply, still do so out of fear of being poorly viewed. And so I deny myself and my soul, in the fear of being misjudged and rejected.

∾

Lack of respect for ourselves, for our souls, simply to garner respect from others and from the outside world.

∾

It is a schema I have known since my tender infancy.

It is the schema of social acceptance (parents, then school, then society). It repeats itself at every outside entreaty.

∾

Is that acting within desire, pleasure, with the heart, with the soul?

∾

That is the question: who is to say whether your actions confirm your heart or something outside of you that is foreign to you?

∾

To love and respect yourself is to act with your heart.

∾

This evening my heart cries out; it can no longer contain the anger accumulated by this disrespect of self.

It screams with violence. It is terrifying. It is the violence hidden for so long within me, buried by the shame of feeling the desire to express it, held there for so long. Too much shame. Too much disrespect.

Today I see how much anger my heart had to endure in silence. I understand this hushed violence within me.

75

No, I am no longer ashamed. I know that my heart has swallowed too much grief, too much displeasure. And today everything comes out. All is being cleansed. Everything is being purified. It is frightening but it is so good to explode this balloon of tears, to let this sleeping violence fly away.

There is no more shame, only clarity and above all, comprehension.

◈

To turn back toward the freedom of the heart, to honour this gift of God in the love of another.

Lacking in Respect for Oneself

LETTER TO A FRIEND

You have masked the absence of love with defensive behaviour.

It is a mask that those closest to you provoked you into donning: the path of material and emotional riches.

You believed that the riches lay outside of you. You believed that you had to take part in the hunt so that you could feel spoiled with objects and friendships in order to feel secure, in order to feel loved. You believed that to be loved meant to be spoiled and sought after.

As long as no one contradicted you but rather encouraged you in this course of illusion, you continued to see wealth outside of yourself.

You no longer believed in yourself, in what you are, not you-ego, but the you-truly.

You did not trust in the love that you represent in your purest expression.

You believed in false love, earned with effort by seducing others.

This mechanism got carried away. Little by little you came to believe that only what was outside of yourself was attractive and worthy of being seen and possessed. Thus, you have always wanted to obtain what another person could own, be, have, not what was there at the depth of you.

That is where you began to lack respect and love for yourself. You abandoned yourself in this illusion.

Through this attitude, you wanted to test the love of another by asking from him.

&

To ask another in order to test his love. A 'yes' means victory, a 'no' defeat.

You do not consider where your real desire lies. Neither do you take into account the capacity and the desire of the other.

He had to give to you in order to prove love. No, a forced gift is a sacrifice, an act of non-love stimulated by low energies, be it fear, pity, or guilt.

This mechanism entangled itself even to the point of abusiveness, of taking from the other without respecting his true desire.

It is from disrespect for your self that you come to demand, even impose your lack on the other.

క్ర

Disrespect for another person is the mirror of your own disrespect for yourself.

క్ర

To ask in order to test love, to give in order to attract and seduce. Here is the inverted face of such behaviour.

క్ర

To give freely from your heart's desire could threaten lack, for there is no sure return of this offered energy.

క్ర

Therefore, the refusal of the other to give or to receive was always perceived as a declaration of non-love. A great suffering.

క్ర

Your life presents you with repeated experiences of this suffering until at last you unveil the attitudes of fear and find truth once more.

క్ర

The truth is within you.

The truth of yourself; the knowledge that you are an unlimited source of love.

It is time to stop this attitude of non-love, stop the disrespect of yourself and others.

As soon as you retrieve the respect and acknowledgement of your heart, you will no longer look outside of yourself to know your 'value,' or to be the recipient of love.

◌℘

Return to your heart and you will rediscover the beauty, the pure, the immense, the freedom, the divine, the ecstasy.

Return to your heart and you will again be that divine being that God created.

The Anger Caused by Disrespect for Oneself

THE SACRIFICE

Anger.

❦

It was sudden and unexpected. Nothing had prepared us for it. One lovely, sun-drenched, energising morning . . . A pleasurable morning.

❦

You asked me to lie to them. 'No, he is not here.'

You wanted to lie to all those who were looking for you. They were looking for you, and you fled. You had promised all of them something. Something that you undoubtedly did not really want to give them.

This morning, something exploded within you. Yes, this morning, quite unconsciously, I told them the truth. I know that this act was guided by heaven, to relieve this suffering in you. Guided from above, perhaps by your own soul; certainly your soul was in attendance.

❦

Your soul is waiting for the moment when you will at last clearly recognise this attitude of non-light that has existed in you for so long.

❦

Yes, you have always given to others even before they could express a wish.

You have always given to others in order to exist, in order to live, in order to receive love, this energy that allows us to live. To give was for you the strongest and perhaps the most natural means and so the easiest way for you to live love, to live God, to represent God on Earth, to show your true divine nature. You inherited this behaviour from those who raised you and, in essence, gave to you. It happened that you misinterpreted the gift. You assimilated it as sacrifice. The dividing line between gift and sacrifice is very thin in you and in them. One must go way beyond the malaise of giving too much with the feeling of abuse or treachery in order to find that dividing line.

∾

To give should be an easy act, natural, obvious and light.

As light as a freshly-picked flower.

As natural as a fruit gathered at maturity.

The divine gift is well taught by nature.

We harvest only when there is fruit. We reap only at maturity. A tree bears issue only when it is watered, given sun and loved, and when the soil is fertile . . .

∾

The gift should be a fruit which yields itself at ripeness. Nothing other. It is then and only then that we find ourselves in the divine river, that we are in accord with the energy of our souls and with God.

∾

You are angry. Your anger stems from nature, which gave too much. This anger was accumulated so long ago within yourself, in all those moments when you did not respect your nature, when you paid no attention to your true desires, when you did not listen to your soul.

Moments of disrespect. Disrespect for yourself, disrespect for your divine source.

You gave too much of yourself so as to be sure of receiving. Thus, you ceded to the fear of not being loved, concealing it by this act of too much giving, going beyond your true capacities.

∾

You emptied yourself in order to be loved. You exhausted yourself in order to hide your fear of non-love . . .

Now you know it. You have seen it. You recognise it. You know it but still you dare not change your attitude. You dare not affirm this reality. There are still some doubts, some fears of losing loves, friendships, considerations . . .

❧

So you flee. Do not tell them. Simply pretend to be very busy doing things other than worrying about those who have become used to receiving.

You are very angry because you dare not.

This anger sits in you, pointed at yourself. Your soul has waited a long time for you to respect yourself, respect the divinity you are. It is waiting for you to hear your own truth so that finally you can be yourself, become free of this karma that you built through these acts of sacrifice, of non-light and non-freedom.

❧

Liberated from these karmic, non-divine ties, you will be freed from the low energies of fear, sacrifice and anger.

You will then be lighter, you will be able at last to receive the divine energies of your divinity and succeed in the achievement of your truthful gifts.

Leave the personality and its fears in order to enter into divinity and love.

Yes, anger is a very good sign.

Anger is often the outcome of this process of disrespect for self, where one has accumulated sorrow in oneself, slowly and furtively.

❧

One day, it is too much. The cup is full. Heaven is fed up. The soul revolts. The body is tired of living in these low energies. The hour for change has come.

Rediscover truth. Begin once more to live in the divine flow, smoothly, without lies.

Just offer the ripened fruit, and let fear and anger drift off.

A World of Power

Man is shaped at creation for a world of power, of control around and for himself. This belt of power that surrounds him is a guarantee of security against fear.

∽

Man is afraid.

∽

He is afraid of the struggle that life on earth has become.

∽

Humanity has transformed the truth of life.

∽

Life is no longer love.

Life is no longer a physical manifestation of the divine flow, but is rather taught to us as a combat in matter.

The Power of Fear

When a being arrives on earth, he incarnates into a body, into a world where fear reigns.

૪

Humanity has created a world of beliefs where love is not omnipresent, total or unconditional.

It has separated from the kingdom of God and has instituted fear as its principal belief.

The first fear is born when souls, divine by essence, incarnate into matter and thus believe themselves dispossessed of their divine creative power.

૪

Thus, the soul, incarnated to be human, sees itself confronted by the fear of powerlessness.

Able to live freely, without need. Afraid of the loss of abundance.

૪

That is how dread is manifested.

The soul's power is the power of creative thought.

Each thought directs its own manifestation.

Your soul thinks, it imagines, it draws in the ether and it develops energies destined for the manifestation of its imagination. Every positive or negative thought realises itself in the wake of the energy deployed (consciously or not) at the onset of the thought.

૪

Fear was invented. Fear came into being.

Fear of loss is already loss.

૪

Incarnation brings the soul the test of the illusion of the loss of its divine power.

Man, arriving on earth, believed himself defenceless.

❦

In this way the chain of fear began.

Fear of lacking energy (nourishment, love). So began the struggle between incarnated beings. Survival of the fittest. Souls started comparing themselves. Some considered themselves 'greater' than others.

Where fear settled in, love took flight.

These souls, used to floating in an ocean of unlimited love, found themselves in a universe where love was a measured, conditional commodity.

❦

The mechanism raced out of control. Fears multiplied. Man became a warrior, a survivor in this world of fears. Fighting with physical means without returning to his true divine nature, blessed with the etheric power of creation.

❦

Man created a life away from God.

Very cleverly, he created the ego. Neither believing nor suspecting his divine identity he created, using courage and the force of his mind, a new, totally human essence, evidently disconnected from God.

The ego is the tool which man, separate from his divine soul, forged to confront his struggle in the world of fears.

Society organised itself. The need to struggle increased. Distribution of resources became widespread, refined, laid down by law. Competition among men was exacerbated ...

Man's ego became the pivot his existence, and thus he forgot his true nucleus.

Thus society was organised: disconnected from its creator; disconnected from the divine essence of its members.

❦

Man henceforth became a survivor.

He survives all fears 'which threaten him'. He is miserable. The power that his fears have over him is enormous.

Few men live their truth. Few men have de-masked the illusion with which our society feeds itself. Few men are totally free of it.

All beings live and experience numerous fears, multitudes of fears throughout the thousands of lives into which they incarnate. So it is that the memory of each assimilates and leaves the imprint of all fears ever lived. This memory is like a devil that haunts each person and activates itself when similar situations recur from one life to another. It is thus that some people find themselves petrified by a vague, incomprehensible, unjustifiable fear. It is thus that these beings lose more autonomy when faced with fear and become dependent robots, acting as survivors of this fear.

This society knows how to imprison our divine spirits in illusory jails. From birth, it has made us believe in the loss of our powers, then held us in a permanent psychosis to dissuade us from re-clutching our freedom.

The power of fear proved potent for a humanity that had almost lost its faith.

Faith in the truth, faith in love, faith in God.

So humans pray to their Father Creator to protect them from these fears that they themselves allocated and created, and now feed on . . .

❦

No, God can do nothing here.

He offered us total freedom along with our power to create.

Create love or fear.

Create or abandon our power.

The freedom to develop through ego or to live one's true divine nature.

God allows us to experiment with fear. He simply allows. That is the true free will that He offers us.

❦

It is up to us to unveil the lie in which we all participate. That means to understand the role of victims that we all play in regard to these fears, which are nothing but the consequence of our creation and belief. It is a matter of unveiling this sophisticated tool that we have fashioned as a defence mechanism and which has rendered us so unhappy: the ego.

We must shed light, leave to expose this unbelievable deception.

The Fears of Childhood

I unmasked the fear deep within me. This fear attracted non-love, judgment, shame and incomprehension to me . . . much darkness, much illusion.

☙

This fear has manifested. Yes, the object of this fear has appeared. Yes, the objective is achieved.

My soul led me where I did not consciously want to go, where the little girl sits unloved.

☙

I went forth to rediscover the anguish of childhood, to be undeserving, to be the ugly duckling.

In my heart of hearts I wanted to be rejected by the world. Yes, on a desert island. Alone with my sadness. Alone. It was precisely there that I ran aground, so much so that I bought into the fear of being thought ugly. I failed on the shores of an obscure island.

☙

The isle of my heart. There I wept. There in my deepest distress I felt a call for love.

I had deliberately brushed aside the social love offered to me, to feel the emptiness, the rejection; to see the unknown where there was no one else but myself.

☙

So I put myself to the test of love.

☙

Unwittingly, I pushed others into rejecting me by showing them an image of me that they could not love, an image that might also exist in them and was therefore terrifying. A disquieting mirror-

88

image. I accelerated the rejection by drawing the object of my fear to myself. I had become ugly.

❧

So I found myself excluded and belittled, without love in the exterior world. I had nothing left, only my heart.

Yes, in the silence of the others it showed me that it was the only one, my source of love, the true source of love.

I had delved into the experience of suffering, to understand that the true source of unlimited, unconditional, eternal, omnipresent love was within myself.

❧

Thus I deprived myself of outside love to learn that love abides in the interior.

❧

This is an unsuspected source. God awaits you within.

❧

Search nowhere else. Feel, on the inside. I know that you too will need to prove it for yourself, to create a painful experience in order to discover that one cannot seek outside, only within oneself.

❧

I see you: each of you will seek the pain of your childhood. You will cultivate it for many years.

❧

Yes, it is a treasure. You will amplify this hurt over time until your life is totally insupportable. This wound has been created through the fears that the world bestowed on you at an early age.

❧

You were innocent of fear, you were only love. The grain of fear was planted in you. It is a grain that grows according to the energy you give it. Someone forced you to believe in it. You adopted it, installed it inside you in a hollow of your heart. Later you believed it, you thought about it, you did everything to combat it.

❧

The energy you deployed to fight it is the very same that nourished this black hole within you.

Subtly, secretly, this fear settled.

You lived it as a reality.

In this way, over time, you have given reality to this illusion. So it is you who created this fear.

It has manifested itself in you. It follows that you have manifested an illusion inside yourself, a good reason to be afraid, an obvious reason to judge yourself, not to accept yourself, to no longer love yourself without conditions.

Love this wound.

It was cut to lead you back to truth. You have been hurt. You have always suffered over this inner hurt, over this lack of love.

You pushed yourself to a place where it became insupportable. There, you cried out. You screamed for understanding, for God to comfort you.

It was then that you understood that this wound awaited you; that it had to be tended; that you had to unveil your childhood fear: it was on that day that you were finally able to understand.

Thanks to your childhood hurt, you now know that the world cannot give you infinite love.

Thanks to this smothering pain, you have finally discovered that divine love lives in you.

You deprived yourself of superficial love augmenting this pain in order to perceive the truth: love is in yourself.

Love now, heal now in the well of infinite love; thank this fear.

It has been the keeper of your truth.

Healing the Wounds of Childhood

I am furious with myself for all those times when I did not respect myself out of pity for someone else, or through guilt, or from fear of being rejected . . .

I let one or the other sap my energy.

My anger is intense; I can see all these beings draining me without even realising it, and furthermore, groaning that there is so little.

❧

You see, this lack of love still resounds within me.

It is a childhood wound. A child's sore that never healed itself. It has not closed.

❧

At some moment in my extreme youth, my dear parents were unable to give me something fundamental for my soul.

Despite all their love and good will, I suffered from a deficiency.

❧

Of unconditional love.

❧

My parents loved me with the love they knew at birth, the only kind they were taught or offered.

They gave me love, certainly, but it was conditional. That was what wounded me.

❧

I was hurt by something which they themselves did not possess, for they almost did not remember divine love.

❧

They raised me, pampered me, spoiled me . . . yet always without knowing, without understanding that I needed that intangible something that is not often found in humans. They too suffered from that in their childhood, before time covered this wound with opaque scabs.

They attempted to heal it with attitudes of survival, self-defence, each according to his ego-perception, each with the tools of his own personality.

⤫

Within ourselves, we feels this lack, a lack of fundamental love, of essential love, of celestial love . . .

The love of God, limitless, unconditional, infinite . . .

This we have lacked since the advent of our human lives.

⤫

Everyone sets out to conquer what is lacking.

In our human society, we search and find only traces . . .

We will no longer believe in it; very soon we will be content with this brand of social love where each person tries to be liked.

It is a solution based on mutual assistance: the fabrication of a new self that will please and finally feel a little bit of love.

This is when we begin to mask ourselves, forget ourselves, give up our divine natures because we can no longer believe in divine love, neither in ourselves nor in the surrounding world.

⤫

In order to hide this lack, some people create an illusion of riches.

For instance, they accumulate material wealth in their lives, making sure to always walk in abundance.

So begins a mad chase for abundance at any price.

⤫

Others prefer to experience this lack of love through the manifestation material poverty and thus attract outer love through pity or guilt.

⤫

Many people in my life believed that material wealth could ease or mask this profound malaise. In some of them, this attitude was exacerbated to extremes of egotistical behaviour.

92

In drawing everything to themselves, they hoped to protect themselves from non-love; they thought they could assure their own healing.

Obviously, the opposite happened.

The more egotistical they became, the more the ego suffered from lack of love, in spite of all this abundance, which was really only an illusion of abundance. The more the ego cultivated this illusion of well-being through material goods, the further they travelled from truth and, thus from their souls, their celestial purveyors of energy, love and self-love.

∞

To buy into the illusion led to covering wounds without healing them; it also meant cutting the conduit to one's infinite wellspring of love.

∞

Today I throw off my masks day by day; I live in osmosis with my soul and with heaven as much as possible; but I still suffer from these social illusions.

I recovered the love within myself, the divine love of my soul, but I feel these childhood wounds all the more violently in others.

So I find myself face to face with these injured hearts, steeped in ignorance. I, who try to live in love again, suffer to see them stumbling, to watch them hurt themselves with illusion and the masks they created.

∞

This situation is difficult for me to sustain today.

So I pray to heaven to aid them in finding their way to healing.

I know that each person holds in himself alone the decision whether to throw off the illusion or not.

Like a mother, I suffer to see these beings, who are close to my heart, go forth blindly into the illusion without any desire to change it.

∞

But I know also that this is a stage of detachment for me.

I must give light without expecting anything, neither their

awakening nor their progress, but on the contrary, let them use their divine freedom to choose. Expect nothing, never intervene; only give.

∝

On the other hand, through my 'love' for them (be it out of pity or guilt), I fall into the trap of sacrifice, into the trap they themselves have been developing throughout their lives.

I give them what they ask for: to be 'happy'.

In doing so, I subscribe to the scenario of happiness that their egos have arranged.

Their egos demand yet more abundance, material or immaterial, from others. And in my fake compassion, I give to them.

∝

Suddenly, anger is roused. It is woken because I gave untruthfully; I participated in the lie.

I cooperated with their illusion instead of helping them to heal their wounds.

Now I recognise in them the thing that imprisoned me within illusion so ignorantly all these years, and which is surely still somewhere in me, however subtle.

∝

They came to inform me that illusion still resides in me; otherwise their game would no longer attract me.

∝

They hold the mirror up to my face.

I must chase out the residues of illusion that still cling to me, so that I can at last live in freedom, without constraint.

Today I find myself in the scenario I once created to mask my wound – but my role is inversed.

From now on I will be solicited by others. I will give by reflex. Unfortunately, this is not a pure act but the response to another ego's demand.

In the name of love for the other, I give, but in reality, it is a gesture of non-love. I have given outside of my heart, the heart I have not been listening to.

94

The heart does not hear the ego.

I gave because I saw the wound and was frightened.

I was afraid to refuse and no longer be loved by these hurt beings.

I also felt in them the profound malaise which held me in thrall for so long. I wanted to spare them this.

It is an act of non-love for I did not dare to speak the truth.

I played their game.

I participated in the lie and so decreased my own energies.

I gave energy without the agreement of my heart and therefore I emptied myself somewhat for these beings.

I did not respect the law of the divine gift.

I gave outside of the divine flow. Sure enough, neither my soul nor heaven could join me.

And this is how the anger has been newly awakened in me.

I was angry at myself.

I did not fulfil my mission of truth.

They approached me unconsciously, hoping to receive a message.

Their souls led them to me so that our common experience could become our learning process.

They confronted me so that they would feel the shock of truth rather than indulgence.

Cleansing lies and refinding the path of truth is a test for them, and for me as well: to see the lies around me; to seal the truth that I already know; to become light once more; to exercise my divine gift.

Evidently, these experiences are ideal as a way of lifting me out of the suffering of non-truth and thus leading me deeper into divine purity.

The Rays of Joy

Beloved, do not remain in the throes of sadness. You do not deserve it.

You deserve to be in joy.

Come, feel the rays of joy, those that lead you directly back to God.

Yes, each one of us is connected to our Creator by beams of joy.

Each of us is absolutely free to make use of them or ignore them.

Thanks to them, God is not far.

God awaits you there, at the end of these rays.

It is the shortest path to God.

Joy is the one and only real key for being with Him, in total symbiosis.

It is the divine grace that God offers His children.

Each time you find joy, you will also meet Him; you will find yourself, you, your soul, your divine being, all that you are; a magnificent being.

Life is beautiful, it is the space of freedom and the field of joy.

∽

Stop living in ignorance, be joyous!

The Source

Love comes from heaven. The love that I am made of is that of heaven. I have come to give you back the essence of your being.

This love is not what we give out or throw about.

It is not the object of passion, of something finite or temporal. It is a gift from heaven, from afar, from sky and sun, from where I was born. Stop asking me for these doses of ephemeral happiness.

No, it is much too little. I did not come to offer you a few moments of pleasure or tenderness. I came to offer you immensity.

လ

I came to offer you love. That of God, that of the angels, that of a mother . . .

လ

Something in you calls out to me when I meet you. It cries out its misery and asks me to speak to you. It implores me to take you away, to the place whence you came on the first day. That is why I am before you; that is why you read me.

I see you, I hear you and I feel this need for love.

လ

Need for love.

လ

I came to demonstrate love to you. It is not far away. It is just there inside of you. Take off your armour. Listen. Feel. It is there. You are born of love. You forgot it, little by little. But your heart did not. The masks and the armour accumulated. Your heart resisted under all this weight. It waited, like a forgotten fountain.

It waits for you. You must dig to recover this magic source.

I have come to offer you a pathway. A few words, a few looks, a few breaths . . . Suddenly you are eager to comprehend the pull of

97

the inner and this immense desire to love and be loved. That is why I am before your eyes.

I came to bring you to the source.

This divine source lies within you. Don't search for it elsewhere. Lay down the armour and let's go.

I invite you to discover this limitless gift, this hidden treasure. Come and help yourself. Come and bathe in this gentle, miraculous water. Soak yourself in the fluid of love. The heart is inexhaustible.

The heart is the link between you and your soul. Directly connected, you Are. Your soul lives in God's country, in the universe of love. Open the magic portal. You will finally receive your essence, which has awaited you since birth.

∞

It is my love for you, unlimited, beloved humans, that instils in me the desire to lead you there, to prompt you to discover your true nature. My mission is to arouse in you the urge to rediscover this sacred source.

∞

You will recover the source. Your heart speaks. Listen to what it says. Hear its desires, hear its sentiments. These are your own, the true longings and sentiments of your being, abiding in your depths without make-up, imitation or lies.

∞

Your heart speaks, your heart loves. You listen to it more and more. The fluid appears. Continue. Let it at last unveil these buried marvels within you, concealed by the fear of not being loved. Love them, they are yours.

Love your heart without fear, that is where your source will spring.

You will continue. Yes, once one tastes the nectar of unlimited love, nothing can stop us.

It is then a sovereign quest, indispensable. Nothing else matters. The quest for self.

Drop by drop, you recover the love buried in your heart. You love anew. In tiny breaths. In strands of ecstasy. Then, more love. Love for yourself and for others. In the beginning, it is to oneself that one must grant these drops of nectar. One must heal these burns, the open wounds of childhood. You have stowed them away under your masks, your armour of fear.

My beloveds, tend to your wounds, recover your health and well-being. Splash yourselves with these blessed waters. Don't forget a single forgotten grievance.

Discover, decipher, comprehend, forgive, nurse, love your shame and your sores.

You shall recover your original beauty.

Love yourself, without conditions. You have finally found celestial love; it is for you, do not hesitate. God placed it in you, to be at your disposal. Indeed, God's love is at your disposal, without limits or conditions. It suffices to pick it among the petals of your heart.

It is a celestial source.

It is a realm that belongs to you and to heaven.

It is your own morsel of heaven, your own morsel of God in you. It is yours and God's. It is you and it is God, simultaneously. Nothing separates you from your creator. It is a magic place where you merge, where there is only one. This place offers you heaven. Go there.

Yes, I have come to show you the way.

We shall meet again there.

The Ocean

INVITATION TO MEDITATE

It is strange, this bulimia; this immense appetite for emptiness and solitude, outside the world, without make-up. Purity, an enormous will to pause on the first breath, remain virginal as long as possible, far from any mask, far from the agitated world.

∝

It is like swallowing an ocean.

Without fear, running to the beach to swallow the sea – will it be enough? More – sun, water, silence.

∝

To swallow the ocean.

∝

I have the impression that the sky is my mouth. My throat is the horizon. I swallow and hear nothing, I inhale, I breathe the infinite, I know that I will exhale the marvellous.

∝

I know that the ocean is there with me every day; that I often forget it and then go back to it in as much need as if I had forgotten to breathe.

∝

Forgetting to breathe is like forgetting to be alone, or forgetting to feed one's spirit with purity and truth.

∝

A body needs oxygen.

A spirit feeds on purity.

∝

You went away to swallow the ocean. It is indispensable. It is vital.

You suffocate in the world. So in your bulimia you swallow, you love, you try even harder. It's astounding how good it is. And you go on.

§

At the crest of ecstasy, you are at one with the ocean.

You are the ocean. You are the water. You are the air. You are the waves. You are the world. You are one. You are infinite. You look. But yes, all these marvels are me, the animals, plants, anger, joy, peace, silence, noise without noise, that's you. You scream with joy and it is still silence. The world is created and destroyed in you, you are still there in the silence, you say nothing. You speak, you scream your thoughts and feelings but there is no noise, only love, you. You are.

You live. You vibrate. All this without noise. You no longer need to ring bells or to feed the din of illusion. You no longer pollute the world with your cacophony of non-love. No, you are, you live, you love, that is all.

To Love Oneself and to Love the World

We arrive on earth all love, all God, nothing else.

Infinite love.

Confronted with the world of ego, this world where love dwells in small morsels and under conditions, we lose this nature and meander in fear. The fear that we cannot resist this lack of love, which doesn't exist in the presence of God.

Years of struggle to be loved. Years of struggle against the world of ego. To subsist. To resist . . .

❦

One day, there is an awakening.

Is this real life? Is this truly God, are we His children?

❦

Years of oblivion. Oblivious to our true nature. Oblivious to love. Oblivious of self. In the midst of this struggle, this forgotten soul, all that love for nothing.

❦

No one gains from it, least of all you.

Suddenly you feel a wish to understand, to explode.

An incompressible longing to return to the source.

Without memory, without clues, alone in the middle of the world. Suddenly there is a flash of light.

A flash of revolt. A flash of truth.

❦

Without memory but with intuition, with the cry of the heart.

It is in your heart that you will find the memory again.

The memory of your true nature. The memory of humanity. The memory of your father creator.

'Go to love.'

Become once more the being who was sent here years ago.
Lift the veil that humanity placed over you at your birth.
Once again become the Man-God that you are in truth.

ॐ

Yes, you are sacred.
You are a child of God.
He sent you to spread love and to celebrate. Joy.
You are an unaware God.
It is love that nourishes your soul; it is love that you lack.
You are suffocating in it.
You lost the taste for it and your path to it.

ॐ

Then this flash of light suggests your return.
Return to your origin.
Retrieve the smile of the child. Joy.
Return to a state of love.
Open your heart to yourself once more.

ॐ

Return to your Man-God state to give to and embellish the world.

ॐ

Love yourself infinitely in order to love the world infinitely.

ॐ

Love yourself with each breath, at each moment. Love yourself entirely.
And let the rest happen.
How?

ॐ

To love yourself is to love your truth, live the truth in your heart.
To love yourself is a form of worship that requires unrelenting practice.
From morning onwards, listen to your heart. It dictates its wishes to you. It will guide you towards joy.
From morning onwards, let its desires engulf you.

103

From morning onwards, promise not to lie to yourself, nor give in to fear. Promise not to betray yourself.

From morning onwards, do not act to please the rules of the world. Act only for your own truth.

From morning onwards, carry out your craziest dreams. Do not limit yourself to what is forbidden. Grant yourself everything, without limit.

There is no limit to your happiness.

This is a joyful discipline.

You are a disciplined labourer of joy, a labourer of love.

❧

In this way, you will gradually become the priority of your life. You will finally savour the life you allowed yourself. You will live in the simple joy of being in accord with yourself.

❧

You will find the taste for joy once more. That is love of self.

You reward yourself with your own truth and the joy of living.

❧

The bursting forth of joy delivers the message that you have discovered your truth.

❧

It is a pure bursting. It replenishes you with energy.

You seized this ecstasy. At last you have understood. You want more.

More so that you can multiply. More so that you can love yourself even more. More so that you become love. More to give to all those beings separated from their joy, from their nature.

❧

To love yourself and to love the world.

To love and to illuminate the world.

Being Able to Love

I know that my dear ones will awaken when I love them truly, totally, infinitely; when at last I have opened my heart to them.

I feel it. They desire it unconsciously; their souls which send me the signal.

I also hear my soul propose it to me.

∞

Indeed, I love them more and more.

It matters little how they behave with me or with themselves. I know that they are God and I love them as such.

∞

This process occurs in me, slowly I revive this capacity to love others, to love these children, these men, these women, as though I were a mother to all.

I am a new mother and I have discovered the love a mother feels for her child. And I finally feel a fraction of what God feels for His children. It is finally within my reach.

∞

I thank the Creator for having given me this immense 'universal privilege' of being able to love.

To love without limits, or nearly.

To look through the eyes of love, to think through the heart . . .

At last to understand each being and his fears.

At last to find the love and compassion to care for them.

At last!

∞

It is an immense relief.

For so long, I was locked in these illusory prisons of non-love, judgment and fear. I suffered as I was unable to free myself.

These prisons were the ones I constructed within myself according to the models of the society that welcomed me.

I believed that was how the world functioned, so I conformed ardently. I dispensed a great deal of energy to become a different being of good judgment.

❦

I needed burning lucidity, immense desire and iron discipline to arrive once more at the state in which I now feel myself to be and continue to find myself in often.

A state where my eyes love what they see and where everything arouses emotion and love.

❦

It is in loving them that I can teach them at last, teach them their own truth.

❦

Love is the only vector of truth.

❦

Love is the only conductor, the only metaboliser for the transformation of the human being towards his true divine nature that must be implemented.

❦

To love is to understand what they are going through; it is to see their truth; it is to detect the illusion that they have created without judging it; it is to offer them the energy necessary to return to joy.

❦

To give freedom freely.

❦

To give the love of self and of others lovingly. Just love, infinite love.

❦

To give energy without compensation, as one gives to one's own child.

An Angel in the Service of Humans

THE TWIN SOUL

I came to spread the love of God on earth: the love that created you; the love that you have lost. I shed my dress made of light to slip into a human skin.

❦

Up above I am a professor of love.

Yes, it is amazing.

When a soul, a being, an angel gets hurt and loses some of his power, which is love, I hasten to help. I surround him with my aura. I fill him with God's strength so that he can make himself whole again, so that he retrieves the fluidity and lightness of his being. When he leaves me, he is a new being, entirely made of love, and he is newly capable of exercising his gifts, of floating in the sky.

❦

Since I was born into this world, into this classic human skin, I have lived this human life blindfolded.

They sent me here without memory, my eyes bandaged against my identity and my mission.

So I had to learn like all children of the world how it functioned.

Strange how we learn to love with measurements and conditions.

Then someone explains to us that man and woman are in perpetual search of Adam and Eve.

It is said that happiness is conceived between two, with the twin soul.

❦

So, God created us in two parts and afterwards dispatched us here, separated and scattered.

Life becomes a real treasure hunt.

To find the twin soul, in order to become whole again.

❧

No, my dear humans, stop thinking you are only halves.

You are whole.

God created you in His image.

You are beings of love, free and complete. He has sent you to fortify love and to live in this marvellous and unique world.

It is true that since birth you have expressed a need for a quest.

It is the quest for yourself.

❧

You have an immense need to lift the veil between you and your own soul, your other invisible half.

Your other half is already inside you.

It is for you to discover it, to speak to it, to hear it.

Find it again.

Lift the veil between you.

You will be whole.

But for heaven's sake stop looking under every stone for what is already in you and in you alone.

You are Adam and Eve at the same time. You are man and woman at the same time.

When you incarnate, you choose one of these facets to best experience, to discover it, but in your depths lie both expressions of a human being.

Up above, in the presence of God, there is no difference between the sexes.

You are: that is all.

Here, you live in duality: you and your soul; man and woman; the visible and the invisible . . .

In reality, this duality is nothing but illusion.

The Myth of Perfection

There is something that touches me and mobilises my energy, and which creates a frightful, gnawing anguish.

☙

I rise in an anxious state. Images abound. They are banal. Classic occurrences. I am present, I play my role. And I feel confusion, despite the banality of the images marching past. It is a confusion of facts, of reflections, of little things.

☙

Everything arrives via the eye of judgment, the eye of fear.

☙

It is a subtle and infinite fear.

The fear of not being perfect.

It is a fear without boundaries because perfection is a complete illusion.

☙

Each being is unique, and therein lies his intrinsic perfection.

☙

God created us and that is perfect.

We have each of our experiences exactly in order to learn what we need to at the proper moment. Each experience is perfect in the sense that it responds to a precise need to understand and to gain in wisdom.

☙

Perfection is found at random, in the natural and spontaneous flow of life.

Each one of us chooses with immense wisdom to have experiences, even the most terrible ones, in order to advance further in life, in the world.

We are each guided by our souls, which are themselves in perfect accord with the commandments of the cosmos, of God. It is a perfect orchestration.

But there is no need to ponder it; it suffices simply to live one's freedom, one's spontaneity.

Perfection is in the natural, the spontaneous, what is chanced.

Allow yourself to be guided by your heart.

❧

Man has perverted the world's notion of perfection.

❧

He attempted to recreate this perfection via his ego.

He resisted the divine flow in his wish to bring forth a human flow.

❧

One does not create a flow.

The flow is itself spontaneous and vivid.

Its life is intangible.

Nothing can seize it.

We can simply live with it, within it. And above all, partake of its energy. Let ourselves be carried suavely from one experience to another without knocks, without hitches . . . Simply to glide over the course of life.

It is a river. We must know how to grasp this immense bliss of allowing ourselves to be carried by the water's energy, the energy of God.

❧

Wanting to reign. Wanting to organise. Wanting to foresee. Wanting to avoid, to order, to work for good . . .

❧

The myth of perfection.

Yes, man has lost the notion of the stream of life. He has lost the notion of global creativity which surrounds him and of which he is a part. He has forgotten this divine stream that he was born to glide upon . . .

To glide over the waters of life. To participate in the divine flow.

No, man has severed his bridge with God, with himself. He decided to organise everything himself. He built himself an ego. He brewed rules, concocted laws.

He needed to be like this, like that . . . Models, counter-models. Value ladders. Material goals. Beauty, wealth, intelligence . . . Thus he cut himself off from his divine nature. He abandoned his boat, which had sailed over the waters since his infancy.

Padlocks everywhere. False notes.

At the summit of the laws is the ego's perfection. The acme of illusion. To be more, still more, better, still better . . .

Better than what? Comparing ourselves with others. Judging ourselves. Judging others.

Entering into the spiral of evaluation and judgment.

It is a spiral where we asphyxiate ourselves with fears.

We suffocate.

We die of fear there.

Fear of not making it. Fear of not being at the top. Fear of not being perfect. It is a spiral where we have lost control. It leads you around by the nose like a dictator.

You adhere to it and there you are, close to asphyxiation.

Man has created a terrifying world, separate from its own nature, outside its true values.

He transposed the myth of perfection there.

Liberate yourself from this infernal spiral that kills you, that binds you to an exacerbated illusion.

Detach yourself from that, from the fears of the ego.

Leave for life.

Spontaneous life. The life that is yours.
The life of your heart, of your love.
Go forth to love what you are, without limits.
Go love life.
Find the divine flow again.
Let yourself glide.

Judgment is a Sign

In the world of the ego, I haven't known only success. Yes, for a very long time I knew the anxiety of being ugly.

Each time fate brought me together with another person, I told myself that nothing would show, but I was ashamed in advance.

Yes, a judgment was formed in me in advance and I attributed it to this other person.

❧

I created fear and I found in him an actor, a silent partner.

❧

In this way I fled certain encounters in order not to feel that.

I dreaded the ordeal of judgment.

❧

In reality, it was not a question of them and their judgments but of me and my complexes, my self judgments.

My aura carried them in. They seized my complexes and held them up to me, to my great distress.

❧

Judgment belongs only to oneself.

It is within oneself that it lodges, and from there evolves into the world amongst others.

It is a mechanism of mirrors that reflect each other and thus feed on themselves.

❧

My aura calls out to the other. He will see it, will feel its call and especially all its signals and messages. He will come to be nourished by this offering or rather by this dispersion of energy.

When two beings meet, their auras present themselves immediately and display their contents of love and fear.

In fact, when a fear lodges in us, it is at once felt by the other, for it shows itself in our aura.

Fear feeds on light, and thus our aura pales and cracks, pierced in places. It is imperceptible to the eye but not to the intuition.

෴

Someone comes your way and unconsciously his senses pick up an invisible malaise, an ill feeling. Should he wish to play your game, he will assume the role of judgment-bearer, of 'bad boy'. In this way he will nourish himself with the energy that escapes from you.

෴

You have found a mirror.

෴

You have found an actor to play the role you are offering.

෴

Yes, the judgment rests only in you.

෴

The one acting out the judgment is there to reflect your fear. Thank him.

He caused you to pluck the strings of fear that you fixed in yourself, but which you believed to be in the other, in the world or perhaps nowhere.

෴

So throw off these chains that tie you to your illusion, the illusion of not being perfect.

෴

This being will reflect on his loss of energy and will come by necessity to feed on it inversely.

You, too, have played the role of mirror for him.

You awakened in him a fear, which he discovered in judging you.

But in judging you, he judged only himself. It is true, he valued your fear: it resides in him also or he could not have detected it in you. It was a recognition of his own fear, which he came to experience through you.

He judges you and he judges himself. 'That which I fear is in front of me.' So he rejects you because he rejects his self-image.

The game is perfect.

Each person mirrors another.

Judging the other is the perfect means of knowing our own fears, our own lack of self-love.

So when you judge, turn the judgment around; ask yourself what is behind the fear and free yourself from it.

It was you who planted fear in yourself, instigated by the dread of not being loved or recognised.

Unmask it. Mend your fear.

Refind your virginity and, above all, your energy.

To chase off a fear is to lighten up the dark areas of one's aura, one's self.

It is to cleanse the darkness that has embedded itself in you, in your physical and spiritual bodies.

Judgment is a powerful indicator, so seize your chance and hasten toward the light.

Detaching from Your Personality with Confidence

There are several of us here who want to speak to you. I hear them speaking to you, all together. So I reach for my pen without any intention.

❧

It's a shock.

I told you, you are about to lose the shell you have curled into all these years.

A shell constructed by you, for your protection, in order not to be confronted. It is heavy, very heavy. I have seen it. It is made of copper.

This sudden lightness frightens you.

❧

This metal habit, you needed it to seal yourself off from the material world. It has anchored your existence on this earth. Yes, the metal is heavy. It is burdensome. It is totally isolating . . .

❧

You know the combination. Yes, Beloved, you slipped in to it. You reinforced it over time.

❧

But compared with many of the personalities I encounter, yours is heavier, stronger, more present; it is not a random and confused intermingling of suffocating mists.

❧

No, it is not a stifling cocoon, not difficult to unravel.

❧

It is lonely armour. Something that you consciously designed, like a disguise at a costumed ball or an astronaut's outfit to walk on the moon.

❧

Indeed, it is the garb of an explorer, specially designed for your mission . . .

❧

It is not a creation of the ego but a celestial conception. Certainly your ego is wont to add some supplementary details. Some safety measures. In order to affirm its existence, it has sealed its astronaut's disguise with several locks.

❧

Beloved, in recent times you have felt the urge to evolve.

❧

Truly, the gong has sounded for your rendezvous with your soul.

❧

And so this metal costume has become unbearable to wear, you feel paralysed. You have simply felt its existence.

❧

Several times you asked to be free of this imprisonment. The bolts jolted up. You were frightened.

❧

Again, you perceived your body, your spirit, your existence, at various times without this weight, this heaviness, this security, this anchoring to earth.

❧

The bolts lifted. Your costume fell off. And you are between two states. Freedom and attachment.

Attached to the world, to humans, to material things, to the game, to pleasure, to your history . . . or free.

❧

Free . . . toward what does it lead? What does it serve?

❧

You are losing the landmarks of attachment, the three dimensions, weight, time . . . It is a state of grand uncertainty. You have forgotten nearly everything about heaven.

This is the challenge of heaven, which you have imposed as your mission in this life.

Your costume floats. Your ego panics. Then it howls with all its might against the beings made of light. It comes to foil the process of your relief. It clings to fear and hate. It moves you away from love. And so it reseals this now obsolete box.

You can no longer live with it. This box cannot resist the energies that your soul and heaven send you. Its hour has struck.

You are living through the last jolts and roaring of this tamed beast. It is also a proof of your promise.

Remember this moment, Beloved, when you slip into it.

Remember that occasion, this courageous decision that you took, in full awareness of what awaited you.

Return to the source.

Retrieve this moment. You will again have complete understanding of this act, of the beauty and the perfection of this courageous decision. It is there that you will know that now you must remove this manifested illusion.

It is also there that you left your truth.

Have no fear, it is not the unknown that awaits you; it is quite simply yourself.

Have faith.

Indeed, it is faith that leads you there, which heals you of this amnesia.

Know that the fear which grips you today was placed into your heart by an ego that feels abandoned. The ego that you created within yourself, the ego of the world that you created around you.

Yes, you will undergo many tests. Tests of faith. Tests of desire.

These tests will plunge you into fear, more and more so.

Testing your faith.

Testing your desire to follow your path.

They will issue from everything that contributed to the building of your ego, of your human personality.

Know then that the hour has come to engage with truth.

Know that only confidence can take you there.

Faith in God is an energy that will let you soar beyond your anxieties.

Today when vertigo seizes you, you no longer feel attached to the earth; you no longer know the road of heaven, of truth.

This vertigo is the proof of your faith.

Faith shall give you wings, shall give you the breath and the desire to walk onward.

To have faith is to offer the angels the task of guiding you.

To have faith is to harmonise one's energy with that of heaven so that heaven may come to you.

Faith is a channel that you allow to run between you and God.

Protect Yourself from Illusion

This morning I am angry, I am sick at heart. I feel ill at ease. My body is heavy. I am cross, surely with myself.

I know these troubles carry messages.

The heaviness is a reflection of the importance of the ego in me, of my non-love of myself.

But what is the truth that hides behind all my ills?

❧

Oh, I know.

I am in service to God. I can no longer serve the ego; I am trying to escape it. I am in pursuit of joy. I am, joyful when calm, or when I read, write, sing, or dance.

❧

Why do I know all this and yet fail to apply it?

I live in the midst of beings who experience and uphold an ego world, a mighty illusion.

❧

I left this world. I rediscovered my true nature. But I am not strong enough to live sincerely among all those people. They draw me to them. They push me into the game. Why?

❧

I am afraid of being judged.

I am afraid not to be loved.

I am ashamed of my image.

❧

It is then that I cannot still the upheavals of my ego.

❧

I fall once more into the pit of the ego.

Judgment has taken power over me. Judgment is still a means to drain me of my energy.

Today, the more I steep myself into a world of solitude, meditation and writing, the less my ego gains the upper hand. However, when I go into society, I lose this strength and drop back into the cycle of fear, shame, judgment and ego.

My dearest, we must learn to maintain the energy around ourselves, in ourselves and through ourselves.

You must cultivate this energy like a flower blooming inside you. Speak to it. Feed it. Water it. Take care of it. Give it your breath. Love it.

❦

When you feel judgment, isolate yourself.

When you feel shame, isolate yourself.

When you feel your ego, isolate yourself.

❦

Isolate yourself and return to your calm.

Retrieve inner peace.

Retrieve Love.

God loves you unconditionally. Without limits.

God loves you. You are His child.

How could He not love you? Would He judge what He Created? Never.

❦

In the kingdom of God, where you have your place, all is magnificent, even that which you call ugly, for ugliness is only illusion.

Ugliness does not exist.

It was created by the thoughts of certain beings who wanted to divide the world. We are not ugly, nor great, nor small.

We are, simply.

❦

You have isolated yourself in your heart.

❧

Breathe deeply. Breathe God.

And look at the world. See the multiple divisions. See the suffering that men inflict upon themselves, with their fears, their egos and their judgments.

❧

Benevolence.

You will be asked to surround them with benevolence, compassion and love.

You will be asked once more to don the eyes of Love, your real eyes, which are lodged in the depth of your heart.

❧

Your ego has worked hard to blind you, in order to protect you from the harshness of the world. It seemed ludicrous to regard other people with love, benevolence or compassion.

You lived in a world of judgment, of competition.

❧

Your true eyes of love were blindfolded.

So you developed your defences, competitive feelings, jealousy, shame and of course judgment – of self and others.

Thereafter you established a permanent system of self-judgment, in order to be 'the best.'

Without relenting, you judged yourself and you forced yourself to reach the goals set by your ego and other people. Thus you found yourself in roles far removed from you. You became the sharpest most competitive tool in this world of the ego. You were intoxicated, possessed by this illusion. You became bulimic over it. With each goal attained, you looked for the next. This bulimia intoxicated you to a point of nausea.

❧

That was when you began to search.

That was when your feet refused to take you to the places illusory duties called you to.

You stopped the machine.

You stopped playing.

God sent you the gift of writing. You wrote. You succeeded in creating a channel, a beam of energy between you and heaven, between you and your soul, between you and the celestial beings. Thanks to this beam they come and speak to you and you wake consciously.

Then you asked for a guide and received one.

You decided to cleanse your being of illusion, of this personality that you constructed so solidly for yourself.

You succeeded in unmasking the game of all games, the roles and the lies.

✺

You succeeded in spending some moments in the purity of your soul.

You succeeded in maintaining this divine essence within you, for yourself and for others.

✺

But today will be the final step back to the truth.

You have decided to live your truth in this physical world where you incarnated.

This is still more difficult. You must maintain your essence, your permanent contact with your soul and your truth in the midst of the milling crowds, in the midst of disconcerted beings. These beings cultivate negative energies. These energies survive and spill onto those who are already weakened by fear. Then they enter into the game: 'I am judged, I judge, I am an ego, I fight, I am ashamed, I am proud . . . '

This is how the whirlwind begins and so many unsettled beings get caught up in it.

Today the whirlwind is enormous.

You live surrounded by these types of energies.

Moreover, your ancient memory gives you reflexes that are deeply anchored in you. This memory lodges in your ego. From the moment that your ego feels the energies, it stands to attention, ready to attack or to defend. It is immediate. It is automatic.

∞

You must know that as you enter into the world, you are likely to be solicited continually, all the more so because you are carrying so much energy. This phenomenon will be accentuated in surroundings where you have fashioned your ego, such as with your family. These circles have provided you with all the milestones, the values of good and bad, the tools of your ego.

∞

So, my dear one, as you go into the world make a wish, promise yourself to remain true.

To accomplish this, before going out, immerse yourself in a bubble of light. This light will cradle you in your love, and in the love and vision of God.

Maintain the light around you permanently.

Let nothing and no one penetrate it or attempt to shatter it.

Should it happen, isolate yourself for a few moments and concentrate on re-creating or reinforcing it.

It is a very strong wish that must come from your heart.

In the beginning it is a real discipline. With passing time, it will become natural, dear one, never fear.

Staying in the Light

On the road of purification, I learned truth. I unmasked the personality that I had created in society. I try to chase it away, devoting myself to absolute truth in my life.

I have made a commitment to God and to myself.

∞

But the final and gigantic stumbling block is the existence of an extremely sophisticated, shrewd, pernicious and powerful ego . . .

∞

Today I live in the light, day by day, moment by moment.

My commitment has given me a bubble of love and light.

∞

If I deviate from this engagement, this bubble bursts and life becomes insupportable; the light wanes; nothing presents itself before me in ease or pleasure.

∞

The magic of this commitment works in two ways.

∞

In the expansion of my purity, love and spirituality, the light spreads out, amplifying around me. Life smiles at me; beauty is enhanced; all is weightless, marvellous . . .

When my attention leaves the light, the bubble bursts and the light extinguishes itself little by little. My heart suffocates. I am in pain.

∞

The pain becomes ever stronger when I abandon myself.

∞

I feel my soul ever more present around me.

Since I made my promise to heaven, my soul and I live together. Its sensibility and lucidity are extreme; I often feel its assistance.

But my ego attempts to sow trouble, to find an important place inside me once more. It comes to speak to me through my intellect and sends me disconcerting information about what I should and should not make of my life. Today it is the exterior world that offers my ego occasion to deviate from the road of love and purity.

∞

It is then up to me to detect the lie, the dissimilation of truth, my intimidation by the world's fears. It is up to me to resist the temptation of non-love, which offers us protection.

It is up to me to say 'no' to the ego, to expose it and, above all, to take care of it by showing it the path of love, the road of God, where each being cannot help but be one with his creator.

Thus, I find myself in accord with my soul, on the road of the divine mission of joy.

Your Heart is the Only Key

You have finally understood and recognised that there is an anger in you that is not directed at others but toward yourself.

This you know.

For so long your life has been split in two, between your spiritual and human existences. Unfortunately, out of fear, you have often neglected your heart, your soul in favour of your 'human duties'.

Deep within yourself, anger dwells in your heart. It has grown.

You were able to silence and ignore it for many years, for you had to be among humans and act like them. You had to – out of fear of not surviving, of not pleasing others. You were forced to do so, for this was the way in which to experiment with the world of the ego, to live it, to understand it and perhaps one day to cure it and sublimate it.

In the world of the ego you established a costume to slip into, a personality. You discovered it and since then you lived with the will to separate from it, to become truthful again.

It is true, you are aware of the illusion in which humanity lives.

It is true that you desire ardently to retrieve the purity of your being.

It is true that you have been conscious of your divine mission for a long time.

You know you did not come to play charades – yet still you play.

This is where your anger is born. You know, but you still play.

This is where your suffering is. You do not live your truth; you often swim at crosscurrents, against the current of the heart, against the current of God.

You are tempted to attribute this anger to others, notably those who bring you light or inversely those who would distance you from it.

Whether walking in the light or playing the game, you cannot bear this situation, for you are fractured in two: to be true or not to be, to live or not to live in the light.

❧

You attempt to function in the middle, to embellish the truth, to insert the ego into the light.

You do it so as not to hurt yourself or anyone else.

You fear the change that would occur if you chose a solution.

❧

The light still frightens you.

❧

You no longer want to play a role all the time; after a few days you are sick of it, you are back to the sufferings of childhood or other incarnations.

But on the other hand, to go into the light completely is frightening because you know that many bonds will have to be untied.

❧

Fear not, dear one, these bonds only give an illusory comfort or happiness.

In reality, the ties that you have knotted around your ankles or wrists for better 'security' are nothing but attachments to the game, attachments that prevent you from striding toward liberty, lightness, light and ecstasy.

❧

Imagine for a few seconds the image that was given to me of your present situation.

I have seen the circle around you.

A well-constructed circle, put together like a network of which

128

you were the centre. Many visible and invisible links issued from you to the thick circle.

You were the nerve centre of a very sophisticated system which brought you security, control, equilibrium and comfort.

A controlled joy.

Suddenly the circle refined itself; the links swelled and multiplied; the circle grew around you.

And I saw you starting to suffocate. A slight smoke began emanating from this tiny space between you and the circle . . .

◦§◦

Yes, what you construct in this material world is an edifice that brings you only illusory comfort if you do not give it a spiritual meaning and reason for existence.

◦§◦

Your creative will is influenced by these two currents within you: the assurance of living with your soul, in the divine flow; and, on the other hand, the fear of deprivation.

◦§◦

On one side you hear, you live with your heart. You heed the signs. You know that everything is in your hands, at your doorstep whenever a desire escapes your heart.

Then suddenly, fear takes over, you hear nothing but the outer and you are poised for combat with or against others.

Of course you no longer perceive the signs; your heart is silenced; you get impatient; you lose faith . . . you lose confidence too.

This is due to the fact that you no longer have confidence, neither in God, nor in yourself, nor in the coupling you form in material or etheric creation.

◦§◦

Why? Because you do not love yourself sufficiently.

Sometimes you have light flashes, thirsts, explosions of joy. But often you cut contact with your heart.

You don't consider it.

For you, it is a luxury, and thus in complicated situations you deny it the role of guide. Moreover, in moments of crisis it cannot speak, so great is the asphyxia.

∞

You can read all the manuscripts on spiritual elevation, but if you do not listen to your heart, nothing shall lift you into the light.

No, it cannot be made, purchased or transmitted . . .

You need simply to listen to your heart, to it alone and nothing else.

Intuition, the signs are not destined for the play of divination.

∞

Your heart is your only key.

The key to self-discovery. The key to releasing all bondage. You admire all these beings who have put their throne in the heart. You are reading their messages.

∞

But know there is nothing else to do but LISTEN TO YOUR HEART.

∞

LOVE YOURSELF in some way.

∞

Where is the share that you grant to the heart's desires? Do you like to listen to it? Are you listening to it? Do you follow it?

∞

Admit it honestly to yourself.

Do not be afraid to suffer.

Tears will glisten in your eyes, for the pain in your heart is strong.

Liberate this frustration that you have imposed on yourself for so many years.

∞

This circle you have created around you is evidently a palliative for the neglected bond between you and your heart.

This outer circle is comprised of your ties to others.

It is a network devised to control energies.

You stretch your field of existence in offering others a certain comfort, thus offering them energy. Then they become your wards, your protégés. They, in turn, furnish you with their services. The network is constructed there.

You become a 'powerful' man with followers.

The circle widens, people need you, you supply them and they remain in your entourage.

This is how you knit the threads of the circle. Little by little, you create responsibilities toward your fellow men.

ॐ

No doubt, the circle is a prop against fear, but it becomes your prison.

ॐ

You created obligations so that you would have reasons for existing.

You exist for this circle, which could not exist without you.

This reason for living 'humanly' will dissuade you from living for and with your heart.

The control of this system demands a lot of energy on your part, but it is not your soul's desire.

ॐ

And so heaven does not light up this work of yours.

Only your ego will furnish you with the necessary energy. Your ego has already been weakened by your spiritual realisation. Thus you find yourself exhausted, out of energy; you lose the taste for life. You are fatigued, you are confused. You fall into anger.

You created this network around you to find love.

You created an external security of love, because you will not seek it inside YOU.

Of course, this mechanism brings you enormous deceptions.

Thus, you brought yourself to the point where you believe in nothing any more, not others, not your heart!

ॐ

You receive this anger directly. You understand it to be your own, when formerly you attributed it to others. It came back to face you and you do not know what to do with it. You stand alone before it. Your habitual solutions can no longer take care of this uneasiness because you are lucid.

❧

Discover yourself and your game.

Cut all ties that prevent you from moving towards freedom and joy.

Retrieve the simplicity of your heart.

Reconcile with yourself.

Make peace.

❧

You know it is time for you to meet with your soul, to reconcile and to live in harmony.

You know that it awaits you.

Your battle with yourself has exhausted and hurt you. You will experience certain moments of grief when you again envision all these choices where you repressed it, where you mistreated it.

❧

If you desire to make peace with yourself, your soul is waiting to merge at last; it waits in silence, it waits for nothing else.

The Path of Wisdom

A PATH OF JOY

Joy.
   Wisdom.
   Sadness.

❧

Wisdom is a bringer of joy, and not of sadness.

❧

The return to wisdom is not a sad road.

❧

The road towards wisdom is a road chosen out of need.
   It is a spiritual need. A need to cleanse oneself. A need to refind the breath of life, what we do not find in the life we lead.
   We seek this breath.

❧

That of childhood. Of outbursts of laughter. Of discovery. Of innocence. Of freshness. Of rapture. Of joy. Yes, of joy.
   The road of wisdom is taken when joy is missing. It is no longer present in the life of the ego, thus it is a cry of despair from deep within.

❧

But where is the joy that I lost several years ago, when I was innocent?

❧

I lost the thread of joy without realising it. I have known it in this world. I did what was suggested, I created matter and I forgot.

❧

I forgot my first divine duty.
   I forgot to seek joy.

133

I lived in the thick of social consciousness, the consciousness of the ego. And here I am today: sad, bored, exiled from the divine breath.

∝

Pilgrims of wisdom suffered from suffocation.

∝

It is a required road. Either you set forth or you die of suffocation. To set forth to conquer joy is a proof of the return to truth and wisdom. Each step is a whiff of air into the lungs.

∝

Each discovery or rediscovery of self is a conquest of oxygen and energy. These rediscovered forces are the clear signs of advancement on this path.

At each step, the joy of retrieving yourself. At each step, joy resurges. It is automatic.

The road to wisdom liberates all the heaviness of the social and ego-oriented world that stifles us most deeply.

∝

Naturally, each step requires an effort of body and soul, but this energy given is totally sublimated, increased tenfold from the first step.

The mere decision to advance brings the energy of curiosity and of mobilising internal forces, in oneself and in the outer world.

∝

By incredible chance, the world is at your disposal, to make you understand, see the truth through your experiences.

∝

The spiritual road is initially a road of profound internal desire.

The rest follows. Energy, then joy.

∝

The will to engage belongs to the hearts that decided to re-conquer the joy of childhood.

This surpasses the desire of the thinking mind. It lodges in your spiritual depths, in the place where you are at one with your soul.

⁂

Do not ask yourself 'do I have to go there?' In that case it is too soon.

This query is made by those still caught and seduced by the world of the ego.

⁂

The wish for wisdom comes urgently; it is obvious.

⁂

The question is no longer necessary. You are marching on, ready to traverse the world, bent toward discovery of the truth you lack.

⁂

Each step is deliverance: a state of joy; a profound solace; a wish to laugh; a wish to begin again; above all not to cease, not to forget to arrive. Nothing counts but this sublime quest.

⁂

Yes, for spirits that are still imprinted with the desire for experiences in the world of ego, these are superhuman efforts, privations, abstentions from pleasure . . .

⁂

This road is marvellous only when it is indispensable to one's life and one's joy.

It is a chosen path.

Each of us has the freedom to live his experience as he understands them.

But we also have the immense privilege of one day electing ourselves pilgrims of joy.

This privilege comes from God. God sent us here to rediscover this one day, through our resolve, of our own choice.

⁂

It is a challenge, but also an immense privilege to yield oneself to truth and to return to God.

Fear Along the Path

What is it that gives you so much hurt, all this suffering that can be read in your aura, on your face, in the energy that you deploy, in the hours when you want to rest, or pretend to cleanse yourself?

Is it truly a return to wisdom or is it a cultivation of dull sadness?

Are you sure you seek joy in these moments of withdrawal?

Sadness of the soul always implies the personality's refusal to advance towards truth.

In these moments, you experience a painful division.

Your personality frolics with phantoms in order to prevent you from advancing. You know these phantoms; they are the ghosts of fear, the ghosts of the world's illusion.

Why not illuminate them instead of letting them haunt your dwelling?

Phantoms do not exist in the light.

Let them vanish.

Return to joy.

Why this privation of joy?

Why this privation of your self, of your divine essence?

What is it that prevents you from living this tremendous gift which emanates from your expression and all of your being?

I speak of the road toward joy.

In truth, you are a being who at times rejects this path you set out on some time ago.

Your deepest sense is simple joy.

You let it be submerged by this malign will to back away, to veil truth.

❦

You know the way, you have travelled it many times, you are an initiate.

Today, you shun the pilgrims and you shun God; your hope of saving the world has diminished. The fear of not accomplishing your mission, not winning your 'celestial bet' consumes the depths of your being. So you go through an internal struggle (on the physical plane in this case), which is quite acerbic.

These phantoms only exist if you give them energy.

❦

The fear of loss is an illusion.

You have lived it. You are afraid of reliving it. It is past. It is a bad memory. The ghost must be hunted.

❦

Go in peace.

Go without apprehension.

Find joy again; find the love of God and of life . . .

Choosing the Path

Each day you ask yourself whether you must get close to your soul.

Each day you ask yourself how.

Each day you know the road but you still prefer to hesitate, to choose 'non-choice', to wait for a more propitious day, a 'better' day.

✿

It is this waiting that makes you reject yourself, and then plunges you into boredom, confusion and disarray.

✿

Hesitation and doubt are elements of blurring: they come to disturb harmony; they come to distance you, to disconnect you from divine rhythm, from the divine melody on which your soul dances with heaven.

✿

Yes, each morning presents a difficult choice.

But for some months this choice to hesitate has become more and more unendurable.

This choice brings you the torments of separation from yourself and certainly from the essential for which you came to earth, your divinity.

✿

Why suffer, beloved?

You have within you a schematic, a model of progression that you borrowed from your Judeo-Christian culture: to suffer in order to progress, to go to the depths of suffering where there is no way out in order to advance.

This behaviour is based on illusion.

God is within reach.

God is there each morning, when you pose yourself the question.

He is there and He awaits you.

He is in the mirror when you question yourself.

He is in the breath of your being.

He offers you truth to break down this doubt which assails you like a hallucinatory smoke.

❧

You have the urge. You know it.

You want to step across the portal of your soul. You have cracked it open so many times. You are so eager to go forth and merge there anew.

❧

What holds you back?

Fear, doubt, human nostalgia, to create more material things before . . .

Illusion detains you, because it does not want to lose you, you are an excellent player.

❧

The door is open. Seize your chance.

Step out of this state of hesitation which drowns you in boredom, kills your desire and gives the illusion of non-love of yourself and the world.

❧

The door is open. Step through it. I am waiting on the other side.

You and Religion

You have lived your spirituality at arm's length.

You, the spiritual one, hearing your own truth; and you, the adorable social creature living in love.

❧

It is true, these two paths have evolved as two parallel routes with very little interference.

Both have the same goal, to commune with God.

❧

But today you know profoundly that God dwells in every cell of your body, in each movement of your being.

It is by the path of your soul, of your purity, of absolute love of self that you will discover the immense, the incredible and the imperceptible.

At the end are love and God.

❧

What lies at the end of the other route?

Yes, God is there also. Yes, but it is a framed-in God, a humanised God, a God turned judge . . .

No, God wears no costume.

No, God is infinite, God is absolute love.

God does not judge.

God created us solely in His image and of His essence.

God created us to experience the love that we are made of and also the non-love, as it suits us.

God offered us complete freedom.

This route can drive us away from God, from ourselves, from the truth.

❧

You know that your role is to speak out, to explain it to your brothers who paved the way for you with such love and fervour.

Love and surround them with your energy.

It is a true energy, which you will spread over this path.

They will breathe your air and understand.

You are their light.

You have no duty whatsoever towards them.

You only have to live truth.

Then, the energy you emanate will act on them in harmony with their soul.

No, yours is not the role of liberator or of a revolutionary.

Simply, you are asked to be your truth, to speak that which your heart tells you, to be the living proof of God.

Thus you shall see the miracles of transformation.

So, loved one, go in truth, go to love them with your divine energy.

Journey into the Land of Humans

How strange that a joyous event plunges me into inexplicable sadness.

Yes, my dear and tender old friend is getting married. For her it is one of the fundamental accomplishments of her life.

Yes, this was surely an important step, the emergence from childhood.

❧

Childhood is ended.

It is not the childhood of my body but the childhood of my spirit.

Yes, my journey to the land of humans is ending in a certain way.

I have recovered the memory of my being.

I know that I came to earth for a mission.

I adorned myself, in total forgetting, in the costume of a human.

For thirty years I lived the human life with a family, a personality, roles, 'obligations' and objectives . . .

I was totally immersed in order to understand this world profoundly and later be able later to help it evolve.

I engaged myself completely in the game, in joy.

I truly enjoyed this experience despite all the fears that I made, which led me into suffering.

I loved this experience.

Now I know that it is finishing. Now I know that I must no longer play.

My soul and I have decided to rediscover our angelic nature.

From now on this is my only mission, my reason for being which will allow me to live in joy.

I love love. From now on, I can do nothing but spread it, to give the taste of love back to humans.

❧

No, I no longer want to play the game of illusion with you, dear humans. I must leave it.

I do so out of necessity. The game has stifled me. It tied my soul to boredom. Then I understood that I needed to stop it to comprehend and discover. Then, needing to revive joy, I left to discover the unknown, the irrational that surrounded me.

I unveiled the wings that lay enfolded in my back.

That was when heaven gave me back the gift to spread light among humans.

Then I understood. I could no longer turn back.

When one retrieves the truth, one can no longer lie to oneself.

Wings on my back, light in my eyes, I left to spread love.

I could no longer play. A few minutes of the game reduced me to paralysing fatigue. I could not even pretend any more.

Since then I see my childhood companions and I am saddened. No, I can no longer play.

❧

God has given me this huge gift of making out my journey here in this body.

I do not need to leave my childhood companions.

❧

No, this time around I am staying. I will keep my human frame and it is thus that I will accomplish my mission.

From now on I live between heaven and earth.

I try to offer the light of heaven to earth.

When I encounter you, my dearest wish is to reconnect you to your divine nature, your soul.

I present the path of truth, but it is up to you to choose whether to go there or not.

Yes, your freedom is absolute.

I lead you for a moment into your heart.

Doors are opened, I accompany you.

And there, you see yourself beautiful, luminous and divine.

You behold a well of infinite love. That is where you are reunited with your soul, your divine aspect.

In order to open the doors of your heart, we must tear off the mask of personality.

&

Yes, during these moments of light you decide to abandon all these masks that you have created hide behind. You leave this ego, forged so tenaciously for the mundane battle, at the threshold. It detaches by itself.

It is then that you find yourself naked, clad in truth only.

There is no obstacle left between you and your soul.

&

You enter the heart and see yourself again; all love, like a newborn. You feel good there. It is joyful, tremendous and serene at the same time. You have felt this sweet ecstasy before. You are feeling God again, this infinite love.

You are also infinite, behind the doors of your heart.

&

Now then, we have come to taste the breath of your heart, with your permission.

&

You know the way.

You now have the key to your heart.

You are in possession of your key to heaven.

An angel guided you towards your gift from heaven.

You are reconnected anew. It is for you now to go there to taste the light and boundless love.

Offering the Truth

In offering the truth, you have accomplished your mission.

The rest belongs to the other.

The rest no longer belongs to you.

If the message is not heard, not accepted, it is not your responsibility.

You have been the instrument of truth.

You can now take off for your next mission, where you will learn more, where you will receive, where you will realise your divinity in even greater intensity . . .

You wiped a shadow from yourself and you helped someone by placing truth before him.

Let him have his turn to purify himself.

Leave him to take the liberty to discover his freedom.

He is in the hands of God.

Detach yourself from this action, it has now returned to infinity.

Disappointing

Disappointing expectations. I have created these expectations in others. Not to fulfil them was to disappoint, it was to fall off the pedestal where I stood so proudly.

❧

Fear of disappointment is the fear of judgment; it is feeling that I do not 'deserve' their attention. It is long-standing. That is what I have fought for a long time.

❧

I love myself in my solitude.

I taught myself to love myself, more.

❧

And then, all at once, everyone wanted to know what I had become. I collapsed. It was too much for my little heart. Too much fear of being rejected. Finally I experienced what I had dreaded for so long.

Rejection.

No, I did not find enough strength inside me to continue to love myself. I lost the thread. I entangled myself. I did not love myself any more. This dose of ego finished me. I hurt. I hurt very much over my incapacity to resist this confrontation.

I still held believed in the power of the majority, all these combined egos before me, who was alone, trying to comprehend the world.

Did I choose this world? No.

But it is also shameful to be lost.

Ego, judgment, shame. That is the mechanism. Shame, destruction of oneself.

❧

I am afraid to miss out on love (attention, affection, admiration) so I rejoin the game, which I previously fled with such force and courage.

∞

Nevertheless I know how to love myself, but here they shake my ability. What suffering!

It is true, for fear of not receiving, I gave only with the assurance of getting something back.

∞

Yes, once again I escaped from myself. I was afraid.

I still saw myself as a miserable thing if I did not participate in the game. I still felt the need for social recognition.

∞

I know that this painful experience surfaced again to show me all this, that I must reinforce self-love and stop expecting things from others, especially not judgment or conditional love.

The Eye of the Storm

I am in torment.

I am tossed about, from fear to fear, from wave to wave. I am afraid of sinking. I am afraid of losing.

✺

But when I am in accord with my soul, I feel myself in the eye of the storm, the calmest point, and I know that I live in the middle of a spectacle that does not concern me.

These fears do not touch me. They are around me; I observe them calmly without buying into them.

I am in the middle, in a haven of peace, without fear.

✺

Calm is possible when I live in absolute truth.

✺

To lie is to dip your toes in the waves, then participate in the hurricane, in the chaos of the world; it is to put a finger into the disorder, into your fears.

To lie is to yield oneself to the fears of the world.

To lie is to want to taste the storm.

To lie is an act of dissembling oneself, from his truth, for fear of losing love.

To lie is to be afraid; it is compromising oneself in the disorder of the world.

To be at the centre is to be detached from all fear, it is to free oneself from the impure bonds that bind us to others, the bonds of fear, of non-love, and of balls and chains.

✺

I love you, dear one, you who are at the centre. I will come to join you there soon . . .

Fighting Illusion

I have chosen to dedicate myself to the memory of what we are.

❧

I am dedicated to universal consciousness, even though I have incarnated into a body; an (apparently) limited entity; an entity that sometimes drags me into the illusion of limited consciousness.

❧

Yes, I am fighting this illusion.

Since the day that my soul called to me, the energy surrounding me has not ceased to grow.

❧

The more I advance down the path of memory, the more aware I become of the truth, the more my consciousness grows and the more the energy emanating from me augments . . .

❧

Indeed, it is a spiral.

❧

One day, a call.

❧

Next, a desire.

❧

Then, an engagement.

❧

Thus, a spiral of energy.

❧

The return to memory.

❧

The extension of consciousness.

❧

This extension cannot contain itself. The more I grow spiritually, the more the masks fall off; there is nothing from which to hang them any more. It is a wind that blows; nothing can stop it, not any screen, not any attempt. The wind blows, it is inescapable. My soul decided that any attempt to stop it would be painful.

❦

So it is. My engagement is also that of the cosmos. So I no longer have reason to drag my feet into the illusion that I have unmasked.

❦

Once my spiritual capacity increases, no inferior energy can lodge in me without my recognising it and crying for deliverance.

❦

The wind is unavoidable. When I ignore these lower energies, the wind comes and sweeps them away, not without pain. These sufferings are only the obligatory result of this lie, of feigning the existence of non-light energies in the self.

❦

No, I can no longer pretend to live the illusion in order to give pleasure. This game draws me into a suffering that I refuse. From now on I refuse to accept the illusion for I see it. It is immediate. It appears in front of me. It is huge before my eyes. My aura no longer wishes to accept.

❦

The energy that surrounds me now is at a level where the illusion is immediately apparent. It is for me then to choose whether to hand over its place in me and thus lower the level of my energy, or refuse it.

❦

There is no space for anything less than love. No to the lie. No to the masks. No to fear. It is I who must close the door of my heart to the illusion that knocks.

❦

To accept the other person's illusion in order to please him pleases his personality and every illusion that he has created for himself.

When a being comes to me with his personal sorrows, my duty is to suggest the path of light.

His soul has led him to me to be inspired with a few rays of light-truth. If I enter into his game, I will become an accomplice to the illusion which he himself created and which is stifling him.

❧

Complicity in illusion no longer suits me; I chose, a long time ago, to represent the light.

❧

When I take the role of accomplice, my aura will suffer the intrusion of weak energies.

Complaisance is an act of resignation in the face of truth. It is an immediate loss of energy.

❧

My role is to respond to the soul that came to speak to me. I will speak to it of love. Yes, I will send it that for which I exist, of which I am made.

❧

He has come to seek the gift of my heart. I will give it back to him. This light is his.

It is a call from the heart.

The troubles he brings me are the proof that he does not listen to his heart. If he wants to question me, this light must flow from my heart, from my soul, otherwise I would only contribute a little more to the illusion, and otherwise I would again give in to weaker energies that will need to be swept away once more.

❧

The wind. It will return to blow again. When I speak truly to this being who comes in search of a sign from me, I send him the wind.

❧

It will also blow for him. Speaking truly, without complaisance, invokes the wind; the wind of truth, the wind of light, the wind of God.

❧

The wind of return to one's true nature.

❧

The wind of joy.

In Service to God

I have discovered my true nature. I have received the gift. I have lived the gift. I am in apprenticeship. I have decided to follow a spiritual path. A path toward God. It is but a return journey. Returning towards me. Yes, I decided to rediscover myself. That is all. It is simple.

༄

To be in service to God is quite simply to be at His service, entirely, without exception or hesitation. Beloved One, I have decided to reaffirm my desire, which fills my heart with joy and causes me to live in the light.

༄

It is not a question of quitting the world. It is a question of honouring the life that is offered to us.

༄

You know that men live out a game; a sophisticated game, packed full of obstacles and fears. This game was created to turn us away from truth, from our truth. To play this game plunges us into fog. It is dense. It prevents us from seeing. It is omnipresent. It is subtle. It pursues us. This game is not for those who have chosen to serve God, to serve love, to serve themselves.

༄

Sometimes, I watch them play and ask what fly has bitten them. I am frightened by their confusion. I vow never to return to that.

I see life as a suave wave of light and happiness. I let myself drift with it.

But it is fragile. Fragile as our will, as our staying power. We need strength to remain content. Such is our dilemma. This strength resides in the courage to affirm our truth, our light.

153

This game was created in order to mislead us. Know that living on earth is not synonymous with playing the game.

᥆

You know how wonderful it is to retire from this comedy.

You have already lived on this earth without playing the game.

Do so again when the desire sings to you.

The New Test of Peace

Today the door is reopened. Once again I feel the desire to do, to try, to paint, to write, to work on tapestry, to sculpt . . . what else can I do?

❧

Life no longer seems vain or useless.

❧

Uselessness was what I felt. What a terrible idea I had of myself. This is the stranglehold that has held me for a month now.

❧

I have lived intense moments along the way; moments of discovery, of questions, answers, surprises, suffering but always of progression and of change, ever new.

❧

Not there. Nothing to clean, nothing to anticipate, simply being.

❧

Simply living, able to listen but living with nothing else, without expectations, without goals. Peace.

❧

I am there where someone offers himself peace.

Surprisingly, this is not peace that I experience but anxiety and suffering.

Today, My being does not know this state of absolute peace, where nothing comes to disturb the serene breath of life. Without questioning, not even a hope.

Hope for what, given that life is peaceful, flowing without obstacle or collision. Simply the hope of something on the horizon, like a lighthouse guardian at the end of the world who becomes bored by his sublime condition. This condition was so hard to achieve and so long hoped for.

※

Yes, I have almost wanted to rejoin the others to act in the play.

※

No, I fled the play; I knew it had nothing to offer me.

※

It is strange, this peace. It engulfs me. It is a sea, a calm ocean that has decided to stir no longer. It is an ocean of serenity in harmony with its shores.

※

I drowned myself, without understanding what was happening to me.

※

I drowned there; I thought I found myself shipwrecked in the middle of a hurricane where I could no longer breathe, covered by waves.

※

I wake up, open my eyes. It is difficult to believe it, difficult to live.

※

A ship is built to sail the wild, forceful torrents.

※

There is calm. A sensation of emptiness. A feeling of boredom.

※

Enjoy it. But what?

※

Relearn the taste of peace . . .

Letter from Michael

TO AN ANGEL WHO FORGETS HIMSELF

El has already watched and learned the game of personality that he created to survive in this world.

El has violently realised his own truth.

He has seen himself in heaven. He has seen the functions of his personality. He has already appreciated the illusion in which it maintains him, far from his soul, far from his truth.

El is a being who lives divided in two, who lives his two lives simultaneously. Moving from one to the other, he exerts a great deal of energy. In order to maintain his level of energy in the illusion, he exhausts himself; he calls on all his reserves.

El knows. El refuses.

From time to time he takes a tiny step toward truth.

He knows that God has sent him messengers. He knows that one day he will live his truth.

Today he looks at his destiny with his human eyes. It is the unknown, an impression of risk that dominates this vision of the future.

❀

He now views this truth, in which there is only joy, harmony, with desire and fear.

Desire because he knows that the world is waiting for him to evolve toward love.

Desire because he knows that his true home is there.

Desire because he knows that there he is one with God.

Fear because he knows the extent to which he has created a system around himself that will be unable to function any longer.

❀

It is a world where he plays a devoted being. Yes, he devotes himself to the beings who live far away from God, in the realm of personalities.

In the name of love, he has created a protected world for his dear ones, where everyone depends on him.

He knows that this is a world where anyone can find himself again; without independence, assisted, without the freedom to suffer or to learn because solutions are provided effortlessly.

He has created a system of devotion to the egos of others. He maintains his partners in the illusion that they themselves created, by giving them energy, and thus he draws their love and interest.

∝

In reality, El built a system of giving and of love in the world of illusion.

Instead of recreating absolute love, instead of leading his children to God, El recreates love in the arid world of fear. It is true: he sprinkles this world of fear with infinite love, the gift of his soul.

∝

In another life, El had already tried to lead humans back to God but they refused. This time, El found a solution, an impure compromise, to escape the fear of another failure. He does not lead them back to God; he tries to offer them God in this world of illusion.

Yes, he is good.

Yes, but man lives in fear, in a world that forgot its truth.

∝

To give love without explaining the truth of the world, the truth about self, is to offer a momentary solace. A few drops of water tossed onto the fire.

Actually, El held these people in the illusion still more firmly; he permitted them to survive there by injecting them with drops of love, drops of relief, drops of God.

In exchange, he fills himself with the love and confidence that he can no longer find in himself.

He offers them divine moments without telling them where they come from.

Where does this love he offers them, this compassion with which he regards them come from?

Not the human El with the introverted personality, secretive irrespective of time and energy.

It is from this immense El, who lives again at night, close to himself, close to his soul, close to God.

∞

He is afraid to end this world he has created.

He knows that he created another sphere of illusion.

He feels himself hunted down by his creation.

He sees the two worlds simultaneously.

He knows that love and abundance do not come from energy used in this world of illusion.

He also sees all the machinations, the manipulations of personalities.

This double vision hurts: he sees the collapse, the perversity of the world on the one hand and the marvel of life close to God on the other.

This truth screams in his ears and attacks his eyes.

No, he does not dare.

He does not dare to tell them the truth.

El has no confidence. He doubts.

Will they stay close to me when the truth is revealed?

Will abundance remain?

El must affirm his engagement.

Does he wish to continue to play the game of fear?

Does he wish to be in service to truth and love?

In reality, he is already engaged in heaven.

He knows it but delays its realisation because he dreads the sufferings of the transition, because he still believes in failure, that human illusion.

∞

When El decided to come to earth, he agreed to slip on a little human costume. Today this costume is ripping. He has met beings who have seen through the masquerade.

El, this is the hour of truth. God awaits you. Do not doubt yourself any more. Have no fear or shame about unveiling the marvels that you carry within you. Let humanity profit from your gifts. Stop playing this game of fear.

Today you refuse your power.

Know that we are waiting for you.

Know that once you make the decision to rejoin your two halves to bring back the light, we will manifest all the help that you would love to feel close to you. Your power of manifestation then surpasses your needs.

~

Dare to cross the threshold of the world.

Quit the illusion, find your nature again.

Recover your breath.

Recover the power of your breath.

It is not words that will support you in your work but breath. You inhale and exhale divine energy toward mankind, onto the Earth.

It is through your breath that you will retrieve your force.

Your rib cage, your torso, will be the field of your creation. It will expand, expand.

Do not stop it; it is your energy's motor.

All these games of illusion have choked you. Rediscover the freedom of your breath and fly towards us.

Lift the world.

Your fear is small, you know it within you.

To hunt it down, do nothing, just breathe and be.

You are what you are.

Simply breathe. You will play no more. Breathe. You find yourself. Breathe. Your condition will change by itself. You have nothing to do apart from BE.

In order to be, you are asked simply to breathe truth for a few moments and to stop living in the world.

You will feel light as long as you live in the essence of your truth.

The first key state is lightness.

The second key is ease.

In this lightness you will work in a natural flow. Things will come before you. You will evolve easily. Mountains will move without effort. Wind will blow. Doors will open. Rain will wash. Sun will warm. And you continue to walk on in lightness and ease, accompany them. Continue to breathe.

❧

If you feel this state of grace slipping away from you, stop everything. Do not deny it. Quickly avow your disequilibria. Return to calm and call celestial air into your lungs. Breathe. Start up your formidable machine. Be, once more.

Above all, dear El, do not give into imbalance for long, otherwise you will suffer. Call your helpers. And, especially, call for the force, mine. Equip yourself with a sword. Surround yourself with blue and golden light. Breathe and be.

❧

MICHAEL

Becoming the Creator of Your Existence

I lose myself. I let myself go. Then I am miserable. It is terrible to find one's hands and feet tied again to nothingness, always so present, so heavy.

Attached to illusion: that is what is happening to me again.

୧

I go on vacation with so many others, so many customs, so many prejudices, so many attitudes. I go off and let myself be absorbed by the attitude of the world. I see it and start observing it. Yes, it still touches me since it absorbs me.

I look and there I forget myself, I forget my life mode, how I function and I let myself be poured into the mould of their vacation.

I eat, I sleep, I laugh, I smile, I listen, I am with them constantly. Something grabs at me unceasingly.

Nothing escapes me and I do not succeed in escaping it. It is that which lost me at a certain point in my life; it is that which had already rendered me ill. It is the same thing that had led me to say 'enough!', stop and understand.

୧

I have become myself again.

I have finally loved myself just as I am.

I have recreated my life.

I have recovered the rhythm. The rhythm of my soul, which I myself so profoundly desire, the rhythm that enchants me, which sweeps me into Delight.

୧

Then I was overcome by the brouhaha of this scene. I lost my markers and let myself drift at the bidding of whatever made demands on me.

Then, of course, I lost my rhythm, I lost my ear, I heard nothing any more.

Where am I? What can I do to retrieve the smile? The absolute?

I allowed myself to be shaken by the spasms of this world. Shaken up, I emptied myself . . .

Once emptied, I was hit again with boredom, straight in the face.

∽

Boredom is terrible.

It is an impression of nothingness, immense nothingness.

Nothing to hang on to. No excuse.

∽

Boredom is loss.

Loss of self, loss of ear, loss of rhythm . . . The loss of joy.

Boredom is the loss of light.

If you live without light, you don't live, you function.

∽

To live is to listen, to observe, to savour, to love; it is to choose to live.

Each instant is exceptional.

Each minute is a choice.

A choice for joy.

To live is a voluntary act, a desire. It is to have desire.

∽

Boredom is the negation of desire.

Boredom is the acknowledgement that at a given moment we have forgotten ourselves, have stopped listening to our own rhythms in order to follow those of others. Therefore, we have ceased to listen to our own hearts. We go off to live according to the wishes of others without considering our own.

163

It is then that we find ourselves far removed from our desires, busy living without pleasure, without truly desiring.

It is then that we disconnect from ourselves.

Thus, we find ourselves face to face with boredom.

ର

Your heart is silenced, now you are far from it, and what you hold in your hands brings you no joy.

You are between non-joy and oblivion.

You are no longer in the rhythm and you cannot recapture it.

You have become deaf, confusion assails you.

What must I do in order to recover the smile? What must I do to feel the breath of happiness?

ର

Boredom means that you don't believe in yourself any more. It is a capitulation.

ର

Your life is in your hands and yours solely.

You alone, no one else, know the key to your joy; no one else can seize the rhythm in you.

You are the creator of the life in you, of the joy in you.

If you do not believe that, assuredly you will turn deaf again and you will be the hostage of boredom.

ର

You came here to create, to manifest God on earth.

You came to exalt joy.

You came to choose.

To choose joy, to choose the truth of your heart and its desires . .
.

ର

To become the creator of your existence.

ର

Boredom is the capitulation of your divine mission.

Seize this sensation of boredom in order to understand that you

164

have lost the road to joy, the road to your blossoming, the road of your divine creation.

❦

Seize God at each moment of your life.

❦

Know that you are God, your creator, when you choose the light – the life – the joy.

❦

Then become once more the creator, the God who is asleep in you.

My Heart Does Not Subscribe to Mourning

My grandmother died today.

Here I am, still awkward in this bereavement.

I have no desire to hurt my dear ones but I do it just the same.

☙

It is true, within me there is an escape to somewhere else.

To flee from a mirror that is now too old and marred, to flee a world that is no longer convenient to me.

I don't know yet how to tell them my truth in these painful moments and yet I can no longer lie.

☙

So my unconscious and I go off to play hooky.

I have chosen to leave to see the sun while my dear ones are suffering their loss.

Why not stay and give them warmth? I still have fear or shame about my truth, about living it openly.

☙

My grandmother is dead, the day is beautiful, and I have forgotten everything, death most of all.

An old lady looks at me. I think of her, the dear departed, I send her my wishes of light at the hand of God.

I perceive her and I give a start, she resembles her incredibly. She is coming to confront me with my own escape. A pang, remorse, a feeling of guilt.

☙

No, I am not a conventional woman. But this culpability pushes me toward an impression of being heartless.

I suffer over that.

I suffer from living between two realities totally different. In one, death is a deliverance of the soul, the expression of departure towards another experience and therefore a new progression; while in the other, it is an extreme rupture, a failure, the expression of the cruel fatality of humanity.

❦

No, I do not subscribe to mourning. I know that death is not obligatory but a choice made by the soul. I know also that mourning is a custom that has been twisted by humans and their fears in my civilisation.

I know that we must accompany the deceased towards God, giving her energy and not shedding tears of sadness, regret, heartbreak or fear in the face of the 'fatal' destiny of human life.

❦

Her soul has decided to leave for other horizons, it knows exactly what is suitable for her. Perhaps neither her body nor her mind could be conscious of that; certainly the rest of us could not be.

❦

I know that no one in my family, in these grieving days, can truly understand my truth, so I flee, taking refuge elsewhere so as not to be false.

I do not lie. I do not want to go there. I didn't go there. They were shocked. And I feel ill, clumsy, heartless and loveless, without humanity . . .

Misfortune slides and I cannot lie. The event passes and I do not want to hold on to it as unhappiness so I let it slide and the sun is brilliant.

❦

It is the guilt for not participating in the unhappiness of my dear ones that makes me fall back into the human condition, into the human comedy.

❦

But my heart cannot accept that, or the guilt, which is that of society, nor the lie.

❦

My heart has been my guide for so long. From now on it will be too difficult for me to lie to its truth, to its desires . . .

The Game of Reflection

I opened my heart to you. I opened myself completely to you and to your energies, for I know we share the same objectives. Joy. Truth. Light.

☙

We are both warriors of the light.

☙

My life is dedicated to it. You share my life. Therefore, you enter into the sacred universe of my spiritual life without a pass. I do not close myself to you. My being offers you total confidence. You know my love. You feel it happily. You feel it confusedly.

☙

Yes, your soul has led you to me as you are led to the source.

This source is ours. We are glued to it, we are the same, one within the other and inversely. This is obvious. It is natural; it is a source of love and light.

☙

We are both its creators and its children.

☙

Your personality combats this source.

Yet it has the key, it knows the way there.

Each time you come to me, the doors are already open to let you in. Then, when your ego awakens and wishes to shake the heavenly energy that surrounds us, it can exercise its strength on you and on me because there is free access. Since access is free I do not know in advance who will come before me: God or the Devil; you or that which tries to ravish you; love or fear.

☙

On your side, you have also left in me the proof of your light. You know, deeply and profoundly, that I will be there to protect the truth.

❧

The game that your ego plays is subtle.

Now it attacks my aura. After it succeeds in weakening me it turns to you and says: 'The light is dim and illusory, what is the good of struggle?'

❧

When you play this game, you are in reality addressing yourself.

Yes, you have invested in another life-sized persona (me) to represent the spiritual you.

Your ego plays through you, through me.

And the game is perfect because you own the keys to my persona.

❧

In this play, You-Ego attacks You-Spiritual.

❧

The game is perfect. Everything plays out as though on the inside of the same being, for you have free and permanent access to my being.

❧

My love, isn't this scenario perfect! Thanks to this game, it is possible for you to watch yourself act by projecting the action outside of yourself.

You activate inner doubt and then decide where your willingness lies.

❧

The perfection perfects itself if my acceptance of this scenario can be explained. Evidently, it can.

❧

God is genial. So are we. You play the ego. In reality, through the shake-up that you arouse through your game, you reveal the presence of my ego, the remnants of non-love that still reside in me which I had believed to be cleared out.

170

You play the ego and thus you find an echo in me.

❧

In this way, both of us are trapped; we catch ourselves in a dialogue of egos and non-love, a dialogue of the deaf . . .

❧

You play in order to outwit the light in you using me.

Thus we find ourselves face-to-face, shaken by the reflective image of the ego residing in each of us.

❧

You are an extraordinary test of strength for me.

When you play, I discover that there are still low energies to be cleansed within myself.

❧

I know that I manifested this game through you to multiply the tests of my spiritual force.

Each time you surprise those energies in me.

❧

I know that our spiritual force will one day prevent us from playing this game simply by blocking the ego in both of us.

Thus the ego's energy will be unable to cling to anything, neither to me nor to you. And we will reflect a light that is strong enough to illuminate us on our road.

❧

If I have written this text, it was surely to unveil the game we are playing and that it is time to stop.

Yes, we must end those sufferings it arouses in us.

This game estranges us from the light and from love.

❧

This game has aided us to realise that we possess energies of ego and doubt.

❧

Surely it will reappear if we desire it, but I believe that the light that the sky gives us this evening can protect us from suffering.

❧

Let us blow the wind of deliverance. Let us lay down the arms of the ego.

⌘

The game aspired to shroud us both in the world of illusion, to distance us from our mission, our joy and our love.

This game cut off the celestial love with which we nourish our union.

⌘

This game has created fictitious situations of dependence, of guilt, of doubt, of multiple and intermixed low energies between you and myself.

⌘

I suggest you replace it now with the mutual quest for inner peace,

⌘

for love,

⌘

for well-being,

⌘

for joy . . .

Cherished Families

You live with a mixture of attitudes, which, over the course of time, are created, refined, knotted together and exacerbated.

∞

You live in this human illusion where relations between people are not founded in unconditional and unlimited love but from an ongoing calculation of several factors: well-being, giving and its limitations, sacrifice, pride, success . . .

You have lost the clarity of your existence.

∞

We come to earth to live in love and for love.

∞

We come to express the total freedom that God gave us at birth.

∞

We come here with a single mission, to express joy and unlimited love.

∞

We do not come here to achieve 'success,' to win, to create an ego, to fight with each other and thus to be 'more' than the others . . .

∞

These are but illusions that the human being has designed to mask his loss of memory.

Yes, we all lose memory of that which we came to do on this earth.

∞

So we enter into the game of the ego, the game of humanity where each person strives to create a role for himself so as to fill in the emptiness caused by the forgetting of his essence. It is also and especially a game of roles to gain the love of others.

173

To exist in the function of another person's judgment so that he might love, feed us his energy.

✿

Each family is a microcosm of role-playing.

Each person assumes a precise role.

Each member creates his attitudes to survive there.

✿

And then with time we find ourselves in a society that is increasingly distanced from truth and love in its simplest and most intense expression.

✿

As its name indicates, the role is in essence an invention, a behavioural illusion formed outside the divine energy.

✿

Acting a role steers us from our truths, from our divine souls and thus from joy and from unlimited love.

To act this role is harmful in the sense that we disconnect from our sources, our essences and our wells of divine energy.

To act a role develops low energies in each of us: on the physical level, at the emotional level and on the mental plane.

✿

True freedom of being begins when the individual has unveiled everything in himself that is foreign to his essence: the social roles, the attitudes and thoughts that follow . . .

✿

Yet God gives us freedom to be in accord with His truth or to play the game.

Each being has this tremendous privilege of exercising his liberty.

✿

Our society has developed this game, this illusion, this lie, so much that it is extremely difficult to understand and to grasp the truth. Everything is constructed, organised around the ego and the race to success.

✿

Therefore, the human being frequently wakes suddenly to inexplicable shocks. At such moments he understands.

ℭ

The family is a formidable ground to exercise the roles and emotions one wishes to experiment with on this earth.

But above all, it is our first chance to display love and perhaps our real mission.

ℭ

Beings unite in a very precise design, decided up above by free will.

A great love surely links these beings who have decided to return and amuse themselves together on earth. Here they will demonstrate love, hate or indifference but it is through love that they will attempt together to experiment and evolve.

ℭ

The family is a cell of love.

ℭ

It is in this context of love that the souls decided to incarnate and come to experiment with humanity. Souls unite in order to play successive roles of master, student, companion, supporter, traitor . . .

It is surely a challenge for each soul to show love in the face of all the ordeals it has chosen.

ℭ

The family is the primary place where we create our egos.

The family is also the primary place where we must rediscover and demonstrate our divine natures.

The family is in a way a setting of apprenticeship for the divine self. It is the point of departure for our mission.

It is from here that we must extend our capacity to love.

ℭ

Through imagining the family expanding into the infinite, each of us will recover our gift for loving, loving without boundaries, without distinction . . .

ℭ

175

Understand that all of humanity is your family.

∞

Understand that the family is a stage of learning to love, and that we must not stop there.

∞

Never stop at the illusion of separation.

∞

Indeed, every other being is truly a member of your own real family, that of our creator.

Honouring Yourself

To give, to ask.
  Such is the ebb and flow of life.
  Giving is visibly the more divine act of the two.
  The visible is only illusion.

⊷

To ask is to bestow yourself honour.
  To ask is to put true value into your action.
  Knowing that you have to ask is knowing that you have to evaluate this realisation.

⊷

The act closest to God is love.
  To love, in the first place, is to love oneself without limits, without judgments, without underrating or overrating out of fear of being oneself.
  To love another person evolves from the apprenticeship of self-love.

⊷

To love yourself is the first act toward God.

⊷

To love yourself is to love His work without limits, despite all the false limits that society has placed around us.
  To love yourself is to recognise being a piece of God.
  To love yourself is to refind your true divine nature; it is to return to Oneness.

⊷

Asking is simply a reflection of giving, to oneself.
  To ask is to tender a hand to another person and offer him the opportunity for the marvellous act of giving.

177

To ask really means to putting someone else to the test of giving, setting him to face his generosity, his divinity.

∽

You have created and you have given energy to the world.

Without knowing it, you were a channel of God.

In order to continue to vibrate in these human acts, to be able to keep on existing, the divine energy must be honoured.

∽

To ask is to honour its coming . . .

Yes, we have recognised you, honoured this gesture which flowed between our hands.

Ask and you give honour to your divine soul, you give energy back to it.

The divine flow.

∽

If you give without asking, your soul will experience an imbalance of energies.

God loves you. Love Him. Do not underestimate the divinity of your being.

You are afraid that others do not honour you. You are afraid of their fear.

They are afraid of lack, so they become greedy; they fear returning the energy that you offered them.

This fear does not belong to you.

Do not adopt it lest it pollute your pure heart.

∽

To ask is to face your fear, fear of their greed, human greed, fear of lack, which is or was perhaps the reflection of something in you that you find annoying.

∽

Detach yourself from this fear: it belongs only to those who have distanced themselves from their divinity, from the divine river.

∽

Fearful beings are greedy.

Divine beings are free.

☙

Free, ask in the love of your giving.

They are free to respond, to see or to hide the truth.

You have given your energy, you have declared its value, you have created and honoured, you have emitted a free and creative flux.

☙

The reflux will come from God.

Did it issue from those who received your energy? That has no importance whatever.

The answer lies in each person's choice.

☙

To ask of someone also means to aid him to be clairvoyant and to live in truth.

To speak truth brings God to the other, freedom.

Truth never creates indifference.

You have spoken truth and you have caused the world to evolve.

To ask is to cause another person to evolve toward truth.

☙

You have created, you have asked, and you have honoured your action; now you are free, nothing between you and truth.

You can leave in lightness toward other creations.

Forgiveness

You no longer wanted to believe in the light, you hurt too much.
 You leave without forgiveness.

❧

Forgiveness. To forgive.
 No, you were not ready at the time. You gave your heart away
without thinking. And here you were wounded.
 You gave light and here you are in the dark.

❧

Forgiveness is an act of love, without conditions, without limits.
Someone hurts you and you forgive him.

❧

You have seen that this hurt is in reality directed at himself.
 You have seen the distress in which he finds himself.
 From your pure eyes, you see truth. You see a being who hurt
himself through you.

❧

You love him then; you give him compassion and benevolence.
 You see with your divine eyes.
 You return to him what God has offered him each day since his
birth. Love.
 You forgive and you give him back the love of God, which he
has forgotten on his road.
 You forgive and you restore his sight.
 He can open his eyes to the world without fear or illusions.
 He can perceive the light.
 He can believe in absolute love.

❧

To forgive is to return God to man.

To forgive is to lead back to the path of light.

To forgive is to become God's messenger.

It is to be God's appointed one.

Yes, God gives His word in the act of pardoning.

You forgive and in that instant you become the voice, eyes and breath of God.

You brought the light back into the halls of fear, you assisted love to win over the world.

To forgive is to be the one through whom God sends His gift.

Forgive and honour your act: you have fulfilled your mission; you have taken care of the animal that threatened you.

Forgive, this hurt cannot reach you.

No, you have restored the light, the darkness has faded. You do not respond to fear with fear but with confidence. It is with Good that you respond to Bad.

It is with God that you respond to this being in distress.

Nothing resists God. Neither hurt nor fear.

Forgive and thank yourself for having seized this chance.

You have known how to sublimate yourself.

You have felt the immensity for a few seconds.

It is a moment where you are attached to nothing, especially not fear.

Free. Pure.

You float in a cloud of love and well-being.

From this cloud, you send out light. It is infinite, infinitely good.

The beatitude.

It is a moment of fusion with your celestial part.

Now you know. You will long to go back there often, to feel God within you.

❧

Each loving gesture opens the sky to show you the beauty and magnificence of God and of yourself.

Silence is a Gift from God

God created us in silence.

He created us with a material that made not of matter but simply of love.

He has loved us in his thought. He desired to see His children born. So they were born.

His workers, the creator Gods, used no tool other than the same breath of creative thought.

They thought, they loved, and they created.

‰

Yesterday my soul led me onto a very difficult path.

It wanted to pull me out of my silence.

This holy silence in which I can hear whispered messages, in which I listen attentively to the murmurings of angels, the breath of the wind, the rustling of leaves, the blooming of flowers.

Yes, it is in silence that I enter into communion with the divine world.

It is in silence that heaven opens to speak to me, of love only.

‰

So I organise my terrestrial life so as to receive the gift of celestial hearing, to preserve harmony in my entire being, here and beyond.

Yes, it is in silence that the soul comes to link up with the body via a sonorous yet very subtle connection.

‰

You have crafted silence and it is heaven's symphony that cradles you, makes you dance or puts you to sleep like a newborn.

‰

To be silent is to honour the love of heaven.

In this way you receive celestial love and you leave to celebrate the terrestrial world replenished with love.

Yes, you become the bond between heaven and earth.

❧

Then my dear celestial companion sent me the obligatory experience of noise. Later I understood that my soul wanted to air the reflection of what was going on inside me, too much loudness between the two of us. I had to recover greater peace in myself.

Hammers appeared and smashed this silence, without respite and especially without pity.

❧

I turned inward. I did not understand the message in this disagreeable happening. Then I fled my temple of silence, which had become one of trial and noise.

❧

I ran into the town. Nothing did it. Everywhere the screech of motors, bells, cries . . . Everywhere.

I was pursued by a tyranny that had no face, no name. Simply clamour.

Noise imposes itself on you without permission, without warning. Men have never respected this divine right of light, oxygen, water, nature . . .

In our human society we have forgotten to respect silence. It is true, silence seems useless. Why be quiet? One must create matter.

❧

God created us in silence, without hammering but with love and the magic of the creative breath.

❧

If you wish to recapture your divinity, your true nature, you must recover silence.

It is a fundamental rule, my dear humans. Reclaim this divine right where you live and create.

❧

Yes, silence is a divine right and a divine universe.

⚭

Reclaim it, organise it, recreate it in your societies.

Explain the tyranny of noise, which in an underhanded way cuts you off from celestial hearing, the hearing of your soul and, quite simply, your peace.

Cultivate it around yourself as you cultivate beauty. Give your companions the taste for it.

⚭

Live for a few minutes outside the chaos, savour these minutes of ecstasy, lead yourselves towards the horizon of silence.

⚭

In the silence, be.

A few moments of ecstasy.

Men Rush About

Running. To be on time. To grab chances.

❧

Know that luck does not exist in the scale of time.

❧

Luck is a gift of fate.

Fate is the divine will.

❧

God loves to surprise you with pleasures. Surprise, the unexpected.

My dear humans, you lack confidence. You do not think yourself wondrous.

You are afraid that luck will turn its back on you, so you rush about.

❧

God created life according to a rhythm, a melody.

Yes, there is a sacred music that beats in the sky, that makes the birds sing and the angels dance. This music has cradled your creation and that of your souls.

❧

It is true, that your peers have created many objects here, machines that prevent you from hearing it.

You also, my loves, you participate in dissipating the music of your hearts.

❧

We have allowed the mind to speak, so as to order the world and develop matter.

The mind does not know the celestial melody.

It was created by humans who could no longer hear their souls, or their guides, or God.

So man allowed the regime of the mind to spread. He has rationalised, predicted, ordained . . . Matter developed.

Little by little men forgot this delicate, angelic music that lulled their birth.

Only hammers and motors, reasons and orders impose their noises.

No, their noise is scarcely pleasing to you.

It is true: it has become difficult to hear the heavenly rhythm beating in your hearts.

In this mental world, we foresee; we count; we impose hours, days, clocks. Thus when a happy event appears to approach, you rush to bring it about, you get impatient, you bite your nails in expectation. Time seems to stand still.

Luck does not obey the mental regime.

Luck is a present sent by heaven when you are outside of time, outside of your race, outside of your expectations.

It is sent to you when you have retrieved the song of your soul, when you have abandoned yourself to the divine river, without waiting, without prediction.

You have confidence in life. You love it. You love. You know that this love that you carry within you will bring the chance to you. You have loved, yourself, the others, and God.

You have honoured your creator.

You have become His instrument for diffusing love.

You have given the world the love that you promised Him at birth, and you receive.

Patience

It is having confidence. Confidence in God, confidence in self and confidence in the divine flow of life.

☙

We have asked. We have commanded the cosmos. We must then allow our desire to arrive. Patience.

☙

When you order the cosmos, you send energy to heaven.

A bubble of energy leaves your heart, your aura, your being.

It is leaving to conquer your desire.

☙

This bubble is a musical note; it is the strike of a symphony. The angels have seized their violins, your soul the baton. Everyone attunes to satisfy you.

You have formulated a desire; you know it is part of the purity of the cosmos, advancing the world; you know it will contribute to your well-being and spread your love.

You know that you desire to spread love.

You are then in harmony with God.

You are in accord with your mission.

God created you to spread love and to live it.

When your desire is in accord with your divine nature, nothing can stop this energy that you have deployed.

☙

So the bubble is in the air, you are there; now you must have patience.

Patience. It is a state of transformation.

Yes, you and your world are rising up to welcome this change, this desire, this creation . . .

❧

It is not a state of waiting but of transformation.

Yes, desire also needs you in order to arrive. Its coming is the consecration of the evolution of your being.

❧

It will appear when you are totally prepared to receive it.

It is not a question of waiting for it; that is a fixed state.

❧

Waiting is a state of despair.

You wait, you decide to halt your creation, your evolution, in order to receive the expected object.

You asphyxiate yourself.

You are suspended.

❧

To wait means to give away your divine liberty of being and creating a finished object. No, do not lock yourself in the prison of waiting, of illusion. Waiting is a prison that we build for ourselves.

To wait is to reduce yourself to a dependant existence.

❧

No, God created us free, totally free.

Liberty is a gift.

Liberty is the essence of our existence.

Let us not renounce it by tying it with illusory bands.

❧

You desired in the purity of your being.

There is nothing to wait for, the only thing is to exist.

You and your desire will evolve, grow, and transform until one day you encounter each other.

❧

Remain in the flow of love, continue to love, continue to love yourself, to honour life, to evolve naturally and unconsciously.

Within the river of love you are in hearing distance of your desires and thus in accord with your soul.

Delicately, your soul leads you on the path of evolution. You have the desire to transform yourself. You prepare yourself in pleasure, without any sense of preparation, to receive the desire ordered to the cosmos.

※

It is perfect alchemy.

So have confidence in heaven, it will take care of everything. Heaven sees you evolve. Your transformation will set the rhythm for your creation and the manifestation of your desire.

※

Patience is a state of unison with the divine harmony.

You desire, you know, you have confidence.

※

Patience is confidence in heaven.

※

To be patient is to have confidence, to know that desire will manifest itself at the moment when you are transformed to receive it, when you are able to fully profit from its arrival, the best moment.

Clarity

Clarity is a tremendous gift.
  It is difficult to assume.

❦

Clarity leads you out of illusion.

❦

Clarity gives you eyes to see and ears to hear the truth.

❦

Clarity takes you to the place where you become double: you play
the game and at the same time you see yourself playing; you have
a vision of it.
  Isn't that a difficult experience?
  Living; experiencing the game of illusion; seeing: whether to
remain or to fly away . . .

❦

The stage that follows clarity is choice.

❦

The choice of truth.
  To refuse illusion forever?
  Illusion is impossible to support when you have been offered
clarity.

❦

Clarity is the first step toward love.
  Love can offer itself to you only if you choose to live in truth.
  In truth, you stop the game, you let go of illusion.
  It is then that you can seek again to live love, without conditions,
without any expectation.

❦

So go now.

❧

Deliver yourself to God and leave in peace.

Memory of an Ancestral Fear

Yes, I have relived the abyss. There are no more tastes, pleasures or ideas of pleasure. There is only ill-being and malaise.

༃

The sun reappears surreptitiously. I breathe sometimes. I still live fragilely.

༃

I have in part understood why.

I have reached a part of the road that takes me back to the light.

༃

I felt the ancestral anguish of having a baby and becoming human, leaving my beautiful, celestial nature behind.

Letting go of my wings.

༃

Yes, I had the impression that I was deprived once again of my wings, and lately I have channelled all my energy towards refinding them, chasing away illusion and fear, reconquering the love within me, going off with the angels, giving back the light to that which surrounded me . . .

༃

No more wings. Fallen. Covering myself with veils again.

༃

I suffocated. My throat tightened. Air no longer got through. Nothing could get through. I needed to look inside myself.

༃

This fear is of coming to earth. It is thousands of years old. I was floating in the sky. I was not three dimensional, in a body.

༃

I decided to come to earth, this sublime planet. Sublime but occupied by energies that are dangerous to the equilibrium of the earth and therefore to the cosmos.

❦

I longed to know the taste of fruit, the scent of flowers, the sound of birds and the beauty of nature: all the marvels that we created.

❦

So to taste the world, I slipped on a physical body.

❦

I enjoyed this Eden.

❦

Until I was offered a choice: whether to go back or to save humanity from its sombre evolution.

❦

I chose to battle. Thus, I decided to incarnate myself among humans.

Once there, I abandoned my celestial gifts for several thousand years.

I entrusted my memory to my guardian angels.

And I left to mix with humanity.

❦

I fell in love with a human. We had a child together.

❦

And my fear today dates back to then.

Childbirth was the beginning of this ordeal on earth where I came to experience life after life, karma after karma, the human universe.

❦

A blind experience.

Throughout numerous lives, I was only weakly enlightened as to my authentic nature. I had forgotten.

Forgotten the reasons for my travel to earth, forgotten my gifts. Some lives saw me strive for the light, my gifts timidly reappearing.

Those lives were hard because humanity was not ready.

❦

Today I relive the abandonment of my nature.

I know that it is false but I needed to experience this event to feel the suffering caused by this abandonment and the failure to return to the light.

A Gift that Frightens

I am coming back to life. Slowly, the movement that caused me to lose my footing recedes. At times I feel my spirit becoming free again. I was disconnected from liberty and joy.

Impossible to bond with my soul.

❧

I take up the pen as an act of salvation.

I know that at the end of these lines, at the end of these words that I string along furiously or timidly, I will understand why I became so blind, deaf, and fragile without love to pull me up . . .

❧

I am raising myself gently. These few lines flow. The beginning of a path.

A thorny path. A path of discovery but of nothing except the path. Up above, there is light. There is wind, which will gust through my hair.

❧

I shall feel myself live anew in the buoyancy of light and wind. It is the state which I had conquered and lost, unhappily, unconsciously.

❧

Lost with my fears. My weakness and my fears. I accepted these two conditions, in order to feel them so profoundly that I would want to eradicate them from my life. They are the illusions that lead you into the abyss when you believe in them.

❧

To believe in fear is to resign.

To resign from freedom, from confidence in life, in God, in yourself, is to abandon your power to be a creator.

❧

I created this event. And now it frightens me. I asked to receive the gift of maternity. I received it. And I am afraid.

cx

It is not the gift that makes me tremble but society's fears, which I have allowed into me and now cover the gift. Thus, I have attributed fear to this event.

cx

Fear of becoming socially dependent again.

Becoming a mother invites obligation.

Responsibility.

This child comes to bring you joy and you take it like an iron ball that chains you to the ground.

cx

To fly away no longer.

No longer to leave to talk with the angels, drift with the gulls, feel like a tree or a flower, become the wind, melt into the ocean.

cx

Nothing other than being a mother. This child arrives and he needs.

Need, responsibility, obligation?

cx

No, God sends us here free. Free to give or not. Free to love or not.

cx

Procreation opens the door of the world to a being who wishes to make part of his journey on earth. It offers him this privilege.

It offers you the infinite happiness of receiving God into your belly.

God is in me and I still have the impression that the world has collapsed.

cx

Chase away the illusion once again in order to welcome only him, this child of heaven. Him and his light. Him and his love.

Chase away the illusion and fuse with this light that comes to you.

A Pregnant Woman

A pregnant woman is a thing of beauty.
  She carries a piece of heaven in her tender body.
  He seems ready to arrive.
  He arrives to speak to you of heaven.
  He arrives to talk to you about God.

❧

Before coming, he committed himself.
  Yes, life is a commitment with God, between Him and yourself.
  The little one is coming to teach you love, or more truly, to teach it again.

❧

You too came to express the force of love through your human frame. But day by day, you let yourself be drawn into the law of the world, created by humans with the onslaught of new ideals, those of matter and of fear. A world of divisions: the division of God into many humans, humans resolved to defend themselves, to survive in the face of the terrible illusion of separation.

❧

It is God who sends this baby.
  He has asked him to spread his light around his future brothers, fathers . . . He is none other than a new Christ, come to incarnate. But will he remember? Will he succumb to the lies of fear and division?

❧

She carries God in her belly and she is content. Her face is illuminated. Her skin is taut and smooth. Her roundness is fertile.
  She, the mother. She, who is chosen by God.

❧

198

She had asked for it when she, too, was among the angels in heaven. She had asked one day to feel the light gushing forth from the depths of her body. She subscribed to the act of birthing a piece of God.

⊗

During these nine months she is but a promise for humanity.

For nine months she carries God within herself, she is intimately tied to Him. So, yes, we must care for her, we must honour her.

⊗

But look into her eyes – you will see heaven light up before you; breathe in her aura, she diffuses tenderness and limitless love.

Approach a pregnant woman and you have approached one of God's messengers.

Intoxicate yourself with the purity of her heart. You will feel the silent ecstasy and the calm of the angels, you will feel the immensity of love that God sends us.

Then approach her, honour her, celebrate her and above all, welcome this messenger, hear her words, you are listening to heaven . . .

⊗

And you, dear mother of humanity, close to God, close to the angels, catch the whispers in your ear, listen to your sudden and incredible intuitions.

Do not hesitate to ask of them what you desire, what is still mysterious. They are there; they surround you each moment of procreation.

Present these unbelievable moments to the world, share these miracles. Spread this powerful, sweet love that you have been sent.

Become their messenger, you too.

Keep this privilege for life.

You are touching grace during this holy period, capture and offer it. The angels will assist you, do not fear.

⊗

199

Humans have been waiting for this since their birth, for someone who will come to blow the same soft air that blew on the day of their arrival, on the day when they were kings, princes, angels, when everyone surrounded them with nothing but love.

Behind his arrogance, in his innermost core, each being awaits you, you, elected queen of light during these few months. Do not be afraid.

❧

You are mother to every one of us.

Become our mother, I beg of you, Lady, give us back the taste for being born, and return to us the taste for nakedness and love.

Grant us again the taste of creation, of our origins, God.

Expecting a Baby

For some time now I have been a sponge.

I am also a sensitive tool of precision.

∝

I live in the reality of the past. I have daily experiences as if they belonged to the past; chosen and desired in the past and manifested today, which takes away none of the element of surprise.

Yes, there is certainty in already knowing of it at the moment the experience is realised.

It is a sudden clarity that accompanies the event. This clarity is also valuable in regard to the reason, the explanation of the things of the world. All seem to fit together in the most natural way.

∝

The vision accompanies me.

The vision of the creation of each event at the source, far, sometimes very far away.

Nothing can stop my vision.

∝

As to the sponge, it is the case that I absorb the energies that surround me. I feel them very forcefully, I am caught up in them as if I were taking part in the life of each person.

Each one appears with an aura charged with energies. They are immediately discerned by my being.

∝

At the beginning of my pregnancy I assimilated them without knowing it, without even imagining it. Then I changed from one state into the other as many times as the instability of the setting in which I found myself imposed itself on me.

∝

Yes, to be pregnant leads you into a condition of incredible nakedness, and thus your sensibility is extremely heightened.

❧

At the beginning, in ignorance of this phenomenon, I lost my serenity and the stability gained in the course of my spiritual path. I panicked.

❧

I could no longer find myself, this person who had at last found true joy.

I found myself again clutching the fears of others and the ancient fears that I had created in my childhood.

❧

I got a taste of boredom again, questioning again my spiritual pathway, trapped in the throes of uselessness on earth . . .

❧

I was a sponge for all inks, in particular the ink of the ego.

❧

The more I absorbed the negative energies, the less I found myself.

I was disoriented.

My heart was deeply distraught.

I have known days without joy, even without the taste for fresh water, or for baker's bread. Nothing.

❧

The scenario was perfect because it allowed me to reach a place in myself where confusion lay huge, profound and very ancient.

I set out to relive the shock of my birth, that shock so terrible where the world appears before you with so little love.

❧

The shock of non love. The violent shock.

To go from God into a universe where unconditional, divine love barely exists.

The state of the world made me regress to the condition of the newly born, who is also a sponge. He is a being who arrives confident, in ignorance, ready to give unconditionally, as in heaven.

202

This state of innocence is that of purity, of confidence.

This is how a baby arrives, without weapons, without ideas, without limits. So he lets himself give.

Then he is caught in a magnetic field that is different from his own. An environment where the energies of non-love come and go. This being, whose aura is so pure, will find himself bathed in it without protection. It is difficult.

A baby is a being to be protected *absolutely* from the world's aura of non-love, from the social consciousness of the ego that is inherent in our society.

A baby is a bit of God.

Nothing but that. Without protection. Without consciousness of protection.

We must honour his coming, his presence.

We must honour his nature.

Above all, we must preserve his innocence. Let it survive to the utmost, show him that he holds the primal comportment of a being, the divine comportment.

To maintain this state is to offer the baby the opportunity to maintain his divine state in this world that tries so hard to pull him away.

Tell the baby that he is right. His vision is pure.

Learn what he tells you.

Cleanse your views, you too.

Indeed, a baby is a master.

He can, if you so desire, teach you innocence, purity, love . . . all that you left behind at birth.

❧

With each baby born comes a new proof of the truth of innocence in the world of souls, the land of God.

Recollection of the Shock of Birth

This fatigue is exhausting.
  It prevents me from living
  Today it is dissipating a little.

֍

I have no activity, in the sense of an occupation that fills the void and chases boredom away.

֍

It is true; I have no mechanical activity, which might pull me out of this abyss.
  No, my occupation passes through the abyss.
  When you have dedicated your life to the service of God, you are totally in search of God within.

֍

Nothing happens to you by chance.
  Each little event is a message.

֍

When you tumble into the abyss, no trick will let you forget that, no activity can occupy your spirit.
  The abyss is a form of suffering.
  It must be crossed without denying the truth. Why do I feel so bad? Why have I lost my taste for living? This is a blessed moment.

֍

Your soul sends you a forceful opportunity to cease living else so that you can do nothing but this: unveil the truth that constitutes you, which you have concealed since your first day.

֍

The abyss has enlightened me regarding my life as a baby.

I was a baby and I suffered. I felt the miasmas of dissatisfaction of a being who arrives here.

With all its tenderness and all its purity, it is a naked being that joins us, a baby who is born; it is a being who doesn't know anything but love; it comes directly from heaven. Even if this soul has known several incarnations, it does not retain the memory of past suffering, so the shock is terrible.

❧

It is not simply a lack of love on the part of the parents that wounds this child, but the lack of love of the entirety of humanity.

It is visible in the aura of the world and its occupants.

It is a terribly low energy; stifling for a being who hails from heaven.

❧

The highest energy is that of unconditional love, that of God.

❧

To come to earth is to pass from this energy, luminous as the sun, to a world energy where fear predominates, a gray energy.

A soul nourishes itself with love.

When this soul incarnates, it feels a lack.

The energy of humanity has not stopped decreasing.

Man has not adhered to anything but his belief in fear.

But it is also a great happiness to experience the delights of earthly creation, especially the world of emotions.

❧

In this abyss I felt terrible shock.

I wept without cause. I wept the tears of this baby today, rendered to my consciousness.

❧

I have felt this lack of love at the root of my terrestrial existence.

❧

It is a sensation of survival.

To survive this shock, to survive this lack of love.

No longer able to subsist on love, except for few drops of it.

There, the energy of this baby that I carry, of this baby-foetus, took me back toward a grief that I had left there, hidden in my heart, without ever having consoled it or even suspected it.

The energy of this being that decided to come is leading me to the buried memories that will be discovered in order to celebrate its arrival truly, with the highest energy that my aura can give it at this moment.

This process is the same for the father; he too will carry the baby ethereally for nine months without the physical manifestation.

My Spirituality in Practice

I know that this period was dedicated to the coming of my son and thus I understood that it was time for me to find the physical world again; more precisely, to put my spirituality into practice in the material world.

⚭

Thus after a long period of retreat from the world, I returned to society with my rediscovery of the truth.

⚭

It was a difficult step, but I knew that it was the right road for me and part of my objective.

⚭

Yes, to be true, to live truth, to act truly in the material world represented a new step, as I had not known or lived this in this world, living only through my ego's vision until I discovered the path.

⚭

So after having discovered and relearned my true spiritual nature, I needed to become it afresh and in every circumstance.

I needed to return to the world of the ego without my ego, which had previously 'guided and defended' me so well.

I had to forget my old habits, my ancient prejudices, my old reflexes and everything that was conditioned by preconceived ideas in a material world.

To come back new and remain true, faithful to my true nature.

Therein was the wager.

⚭

Evidently it was not without snags.

Thus I could see shame resurge, along with the fear of being rejected, fear of disappointment, fear of emptiness and the feeling of being alone, 'outside of goings-on'.

On several occasions I fell into the traps of the ego, such as a return to competition, the subtle and imperceptible desire for power or seduction, the temptation to fall in with the game of the ego . . .

Yes, I plunged back into the pit but I had the marvellous capacity to see, to see the game I played clearly.

I played at ego and I saw it.

I knew that I could stop it at any moment, but I certainly felt the desire to play again, and learn a bit more about myself.

୶

These experiences taught me about myself, about the residual ego in me, and especially gave clues for continuing along the road of purification of my being.

୶

In some way, I have experienced the 'practical' aspect of my spirituality.

This step involved a fight at every moment, because I was living in a social context where I was open to human experiences and to human exchanges without the screen or separation that I had during my apprenticeship.

୶

A battle against my ego; I had to impose new discipline on myself and respect it.

What is it that this experience, this event, this being wanted to show me about myself?

What is it that they try to make me experience and discover?

Why do I respond to the game by playing it?

Am I responsible for it?

How did I arouse it?

How can I walk away from it?

How can I bring the light into this masquerade for myself and for others?

୶

209

But I also had to seize the other side of this experience.

At each moment I had to find and understand my heart's choice.

For each simple choice, I asked my heart and the Spirit where the truth was, what my real desire was.

At each moment I tried to live in the divine flow.

I tried to understand all the signs and symbols that appeared before me.

This period was really a test as to whether I could put into the practice that which I had decided to be, that is to say, myself.

Me once again in the spiritual world, me once again in the material world.

Without distinction.

Without separation.

Sublimating the Material World

I lived for a time back in materiality.

I believed I lived far away, distanced from myself, from my profound nature, from my spirituality. I believed that there were two worlds, that of the body and that of spirit. I believed that here we live as humans and that above we were light.

◌

Then God sent me the indispensable experience of the fusion of these two states, of these lives.

◌

There is no separation, there is only one whole.

I have lived the path of discovery, of light, initiation.

I have loved life.

I have loved the world as I finally have understood it.

◌

I saw the error of humanity and I fled.

Thus I left to discover my soul, to discover my divine presence. I lived in a spiritual dimension where I recovered certain of my divine gifts.

Happy in the world of love, I didn't conceive a return to material life, human life; I refused every attempt to draw me back into it.

No, I did not want to fall again into the world of the ego, the world of differentiation and competition.

I felt free, light on my cloud.

God then sent me this experience of return to the physical world.

◌

My son arrived.

I felt an anchoring in me, an anchoring to earth.

211

I was torn between the immense joy of giving birth and the terrible anguish of returning to the world of humans.

I no longer believed in society as I had left it, I was waiting for it to change.

☙

But it was my experience that could change it.

Surely I had not incarnated on earth simply to live the experience of returning to the truth of my being.

☙

The sublime spiritual path that I had lived away from this world was only a debut of my presence on earth.

☙

To discover myself was certainly fundamental but surely not the only outcome of my terrestrial life. This discovery was the fruit and the goal of several of my previous lives.

☙

So this experience took me back to humanity despite myself, out of love of the child.

☙

I felt a ripping, a terrible violence.

Yes, I came back to live among humans and I saw, I felt this lack of love in their hearts.

So it happened that little by little I returned to live among them, but as a new me with another perspective on the world. I came back to live among them with the eyes of love.

☙

I have often been imbalanced in my quest for purity, for my ancient egotistical reflexes were fired up in the face of the aggression inflicted on me by the human world.

Of course, I suffered on my return as I felt myself to be alone in their midst, no longer sharing the same values or the same points of reference.

☙

Then I understood that this was the test: to remain pure, to diffuse love, to resist the world's ego as well as my own.

Yes, there was the true test.

To remain myself in the midst of humanity.

To stay in the middle of the typhoon and diffuse light.

To answer mistakes with truth despite failure, despite refusal, rejection, judgment and above all, non-love.

※

There is the real test in matter: to sublimate the material.

To give it back love.

To live spiritually on the material plane.

To live materially on the spiritual plane.

To make them one.

To retrieve fusion.

To understand the mirroring effect between these two aspects of life.

To rediscover the alchemy which fuses them, which transforms them into one another and back again. Lead into gold. The physical body into the spiritual body. Man into angel, and back.

To sublimate matter is the second milestone on the road.

※

The first was the return to the light, to truth, to the rediscovery of God in myself.

The return gives you understanding of the world, of its creation, of the earthbound passage of beings . . .

※

It is the stage of the rediscovery of love.

※

The second stage is the 'practical application' of this discovery through the return to the three-dimensional world.

It is a step made of the gift of love.

You have learned (relearned) that you were all love and that now is the moment to give it out, manifest it, exchange it.

It is also an important occasion for testing and re-enforcing the purity one has acquired along the path.

∞

This is the stage of manifestation of one's spiritual being.

This is who I am, so I manifest myself on this planet according to my deepest desires and my divine gifts in accord with the divine plan.

∞

Manifestation . . .
     Then creation . . .

The Return to the City

I have lived a long period of withdrawal from the world, I learned much about my life, my essence.

❧

I have finally found myself in my role as a servant of God.

❧

Then a heaven gave me a period of intense peace, which was difficult to grasp and appreciate in the beginning.

❧

Today I am again at the outset of an active period.

❧

I need discernment, wisdom and to hear God in order not to fall back into some frenzy, onto a wrong path, a mind-created project outside of my essence.

Open Your Heart to your Mission

I take up my pen to write to you, because I know that my words will deliver you from the ties that bind your wings and prevent you from flying off.

঵

You made the decision to be in God's service long ago, before the trees were born.

঵

You came to create the world. You came to incarnate here. You came to make the most of it. Then you came to save the world that you love so.

঵

You donned the human costume but you have known since birth that this habit hides your true nature.

঵

In order to render service to humanity you blended with it.

You created a physical body, an emotional body and a mental body for yourself.

You told yourself a tale of human life and from then on you lived it.

This costume is nothing but a costume.

঵

To better understand humans, you lost your memory for a while.

The more time passes, the more your soul presses you to remember.

The more your habit tightens, the more its presence is evident.

঵

Your costume, in particular your mental aspect, knows that you are no longer duped. They know that you are about to abandon

216

them. So they assail you. They stand up to you. They shut you up. They are there to show you the drift of humanity but also to test your true nature.

They are trying to hold you back from recovering your memory.

These are aptitude tests to recover your mission, to find again your identity right here, God on earth.

❧

Today you put yourself to the test for you are about to once more become a great enlightener of this world.

You are at the centre of the gift of manifestation.

You are at the centre of divine abundance.

More is asked of you at each stage. The vector is increasingly powerful.

❧

Marvellously, you never refuse your role, despite your tyrannical mind that leads you to doubt.

Doubt the lack, doubt the manifestation.

❧

But by grace of the strength of your soul, of your heart, to which you listen very little during such moments of doubt, you come back to your mission.

❧

The joy can be read on your face.

You radiate. It is magnificent.

❧

Beloved, I take up my pen because of two parts of this process.

❧

Know that your heart is crying for help and that you hear it but little. I see it suffer.

It is powerful but you stifle it.

You are afraid of it.

You know that when it takes command, things will explode.

You fear that you cannot afford that.

Do you think that God has given you a huge heart without any power?

When God gives Himself, He gives totally.

The power of the heart is phenomenal.

Its force is love.

It is the greatest power in creation, in the cosmos.

It is the breath of God.

This very same breath passes through your heart, through the centre of your being.

And it is also what created the world and the universe . . .

✧

Love is creative energy.

To have heart does not mean to be sentimental or emotional. It is not only a blissful energy.

✧

It is the energy of creation, the highest in vibration.

Do not deceive yourself as to the quality and the force of that which fills you.

✧

Try to pay more attention to he who bears God within; you, who bear the force of creation.

It is true; you often listen to your mind, which brings you back under its control.

✧

The mind tells you that nothing occurs miraculously; that we must suffer in order to build.

That is false, beloved: when one acts out of love, God is in command.

This is also true: walking through life without God means walking without eyes, swimming upstream.

✧

To hear your heart, you must stop believing in the laws of the mental world, the world of the ego, the world of matter.

❦

Quiet them for a few moments to retrieve the breath of your heart.

❦

In the beginning, this will be a tough discipline, for the mind is very powerful in our world.

❦

Today it is your duty to find peace once more, to put your foot again into the track of the path.

❦

Your celestial masters and helpers ask this of you.

They await the hour where you will experience release from all conflicting forces, the letting go of your ties.

❦

The second matter is inherent in the first.

❦

Beloved, your process of trust in God is unfortunately obstructed by a mental vision of your mission.

❦

When a mission is proposed to you, you accept it and think you are fulfilling your role. From that moment you decide to take all things in hand.

You accept the mission and then cut the connection with the director, God. You 'shut the door to Him' in some way and you take over the responsibility to get there by yourself.

From then on God is no longer a participant in the system.

Your mission now becomes a battleground where, from time to time, you pray to God to assist you. In reality, you have raised a pickaxe and hammer, thinking that that was what was asked of you.

❦

Beloved, God asked you to help Him restore the earth from its ruin. You decided to do that, but please do not participate in this harm, believing you can combat it.

❦

When God sends you, He employs you as His envoy, His instrument, His substitute.

When you accept the mission, let Him do.

❧

Let Him participate.

Do not close the door on Him by working alone with material energies; you will be unable to channel divine energy in this way.

If God sends you into this world, it is to shower the world with His light and His love.

You are a vehicle of God.

❧

A mission is not a punishment or an unbearable load.

A mission is an act of grace where you choose to be the instrument of God, where you give yourself over to the light.

❧

Often you believe that God cannot lead you to what you need here below without your intervention.

How has He created the rest? Simply by loving, in the materialisation of His love.

Give the Creator your trust.

Allow Him each day to bring you what you need to express your divinity on earth, to fulfil your mission.

How?

Come back to your heart. Return to the perception of road-signs on the path.

❧

Know that the doors will open before you want to pass through them.

❧

That is your sign from God.

❧

Do not forget, well-beloved, 'easily and without effort'.

Give your heart and your universe to God, so that He can bestow on you what you deserve.

Our Dream of Spreading the Light

What is our dream? What do our hearts say? What is the divine wish we carry in us, to which we send our etheric energy? What is this creation that we concoct in the hollow of our hearts, from heaven?

☙

We have for a long time known ourselves to be in service to God.

As to myself, I have dedicated my human life to Him, I declared myself to be at His service which is actually a pure delight.

Yes, to be in the service of God, in His flow and His energy, is by essence an existence of joy, for it is an existence uniquely dictated by the heart.

☙

God inhabits our hearts.

It is in the middle of the heart where our divine nature, our true essence and thus our direct and permanent contact with Him are found.

☙

Our wish is to open up, to spill the light so that love can find its space once more like a river displaced from its bed.

☙

Yes, love must run once again through the world, through the hearts, nourishing anew our lands, rendering them fertile.

☙

This aridity, the blindness of the world toward this aridity, must come to an end. We have to pull away from a society which favours the dictatorship of the mind, the standard of the ego and the differentiation between beings.

☙

221

To return to the heart. Quite simply.

⁂

Man needs to recover his knowingness, his true nature.

He forgot.

He must find the memory of his birth, of his virginity. It is through information and energy that we know how to do it.

⁂

To spread our energy and live our truth in the middle of them.

⁂

To spread the truth.

To wait for it to chime in their hearts, awakening them forever.

This is our desire.

A heartfelt desire is nothing other than a mission or exercise of a gift, or both at once if one becomes aware of the divine Allness and perfection.

⁂

We have clothed this desire with desires for manifestation and materialisation, in order to enter the physical reality of world and humanity.

⁂

We know that this project will come to a successful end and we are waiting for the energies to be reunited, for the chance to bring us there . . .

222

Our Mission of Truth

We gather together through love. The love that unites us is celestial.

꼭

Through our union, we are its terrestrial manifestation.

꼭

Sometimes our beings strain to sublimate it here.

꼭

We are beings who have come to earth through the experience of incarnation.

This physical incarnation takes us through life on earth through the experience of limited consciousness, through the experience of the ego.

꼭

The world of the ego has welcomed us in fear.

It is why we have engaged in combat for years.

The battle of light.

We know that fear is an illusion created in order to dominate humanity.

We know it and, above all, we have the desire to reveal it.

꼭

It is our mission. Our mission is that of truth. Our mission is that of memory.

Our mission starts at the centre, inside ourselves.

꼭

It is in recovering our own memories, our own light, that we will at last be able to illuminate the world.

Yes, we came to remove the veil that we consented to wear in this life.

꼭

To remove this veil.

That is our mission.

Then we shall be living examples of the truth, of light.

We have nothing to do other than rediscover our divinity.

∞

Then the demonstration will be evident.

∞

Then the energy that emanates from each one of us will be potent enough to shatter the lie, to cause the masks to drop, to incite others to search for their truth.

∞

Today we are standing on the threshold of a profound discovery of our beings.

We are in the throes of transformation.

∞

We are experiencing the revolt of the forces of non-light within us, which we have given our attention, and sometimes our adoration or submission.

∞

These forces are rebelling, as they no longer own the keys to the city.

They are the forces of the ego, of non-love, of illusion.

We feel the groans and miasmas of their being stripped bare. It is wrenching.

These miasmas reverberate through our beings.

∞

These miasmas act through doubt.

∞

Doubt.

The shaking up of the truth.

Consciousness reduced to fear.

Disconnection with our souls.

∞

Now let us look at these moments of change.

And allow these forces to detach.

Let us thank them for the wisdom by which we have been enriched.

Let us fill the freed spaces within, by the light of our souls.

And let us go forth to illumine the world with celestial light . . .

Rediscovering the Heart's Fantasies

You helped me to realise myself, you pushed me toward this gift that drew me but also frightened me.

❧

I only half-believed it; however, I found an immense joy there.

❧

You have been a warrior against my doubt, against my fear of deceiving myself, of being ridiculous, of not following the path.

❧

Today, I am returning this essential service that you rendered me.

❧

Yes, I am pushing you toward that which you love, toward that which brings you joy.

❧

Ask yourself, which road should you take to return to joy?
   What are your craziest dreams?

❧

I give you the good news that this is your next step.

❧

You became aware that your life is currently stifling you. You woke up to this, which is nearly enough.

❧

It is enough to be yourself from now on, the situation will unravel by itself . . .

❧

Rediscover the fantasy of your heart.

Dream and Create

To dream. To be.

Dreams are the conception of our desires.

❧

We dream, we let go without constraints, we love, we imagine, we create an image of what we desire.

We dream, everything is possible.

We are in the exclusive domain of desire.

Desire without limits. Desire without prejudice. Desire without fear or judgment.

Fear and judgment do not exist in the dream, or else the dream dissolves.

We dream, we are untied, we are unfettered, we love ourselves, we love.

We love, then we build.

We give our desires importance .

We lets our imaginations loose, and they become unbridled.

We can go to the utmost with our craziest desires. The infinite. God. Love. The dream.

❧

We dream, we pray, we give out energy, creation is launched.

❧

We dream and we choose whether or not to believe in it. We dream, and we choose whether to give ourselves the object of our dreams.

❧

Yes, dear humans, you love, you dream but you do not often believe in it, you do not think you are 'worthy of', or 'deserving of', or 'capable of' . . .

You dream and you block the realisation of your dreams.

227

When you do not believe in it, you block the energy required for the realisation of your desires.

❦

Manifestation.

To see a dream manifesting itself simply means to imagine, to love and to construct ethereally in detail, then to love and believe in it.

To believe in it is to send your divine, etheric energy of creation so that you can have confidence.

❦

Dream and create.

❦

Do not block your desires with the illusion of the 'impossible'.

❦

The impossible is the realm of fear, of judgment, of unconfidence in oneself and unconfidence in heaven.

❦

Trusting and letting go.

Yes, you have dreamed, you have spiritually constructed your desires and you believe in them, you trust heaven and yourselves . . . Now you only have to let the miracle happen.

One dream, confidence, love . . . Manifestation.

❦

Above all, do not get hung up on expectation; there again you could block the manifestation.

Expectation is a sign of unconfidence.

❦

Heaven and souls work in divine energy and divine flow. Let them do so.

They know. They guard.

They will call you if they need you. They will give you a sign when your dreams are realised.

Come then and only then to pick the flower desired for so long, already forgotten.

Give yourself to the dream.

No obligation will be able to deter your spirit.

Your spirit is free.

Your body breathes.

You retrieve your virginity.

Let yourself glide through your craziest dreams.

Allow yourself to love; love life as the newborn; ask of life without fears, without prejudices . . .

Without expecting, as freely as the whispering wind . . .

Blow life into yourself.

Unexpected, free, spontaneous, surprising, merry, smiling, feathery and light as quicksilver.

The Bubble of Creation

You are a sphere, smooth and pure,
  an aura of white energy,
  you stay with yourself,
  you raise your white energy,
  the movement is soft, it glides; the sound is sweet and delicate.
  An angelic well-being.

ॐ

Then your soul urges you to create, an idea comes, a desire . . .

ॐ

The sphere glides and turns gracefully,
  energy increases,
  ideas spread, the energy detaches itself,
  then entities detach from you,
  the vibration leads them farther to visit other ideas, other souls,
other skies
  to complete themselves, to exist,
  the souls will come to add their energy,
  celestial aides will guide this little baby.

ॐ

There, you have been the prop for a new energy, you have been
God in the space of a second, you found your real, divine nature
in the blink of an eye.

ॐ

This miniscule particle will join others that float in the same
direction, out of love; the same energy animates them.

ॐ

This new sphere will come to knock against some and others,
  it will leave with more energy or

it will have shaken up those beings who have forgotten or

it will have shocked the poor energies, then

it will know which homes are open, closed, positive, harmful or fertile,

fertile for a pure objective, a mission of soul or

a gray objective, an ego's bet, an objective of agitation; a lesson awaits them . . .

∾

This small bubble of bliss will come knocking at many doors.

∾

And so you will see them, meet each other here and there, knock into each other in space, love each other, detest each other . . . each one with a role, all with a project of growth, all with a lesson, an opportunity to find yourself again, to understand a little bit of yourself, to cooperate with the advancement of the world . . .

∾

Then all these beings encounter one another, surely 'by chance', at work, in school, in a building, at the baker's, in the street, on the aeroplane . . .

∾

Oh my God, what a coincidence!

That's curious, I thought of the same thing!

That's unbelievable, I had that idea this morning!

That was my craziest dream, my childhood dream!

∾

Magic is afoot. The whole world is finally dreaming!

∾

At last they will touch the reality of this world, which is to create.

∾

A desire. An energy. A vibration.

An idea. A bubble.

Energy. Different energies.

Love . . .

A project.

231

Beware the egos. Beware the mind. Free yourselves.

Let pure energy surround the project.

It will float. Structures are being prepared.

The energy is beautiful. The ideas are in place. The project is complete.

It will lodge in this structure that awaited it and everything will unfold naturally, without effort . . .

This is the manifestation of energy.

The Creative Power of Thought

It is time for you to open your consciousness to the power of intentions and thought.

From now on, this power waits to be recognised in you.

※

Your thought is creative.

It is there for all that your imagination can produce.

I have come to give you the keys.

※

First of all, **confidence**.

You have already discarded many masks that prevented you from being true.

You are searching for your divinity. You are on the path. You engaged yourself in the service of our creator.

Doors will open.

Now you are ready to open yourself to another level of consciousness, to realise the long forgotten power of your thoughts.

※

Next, **the breath**.

Inhale your will, inhale your intention.

Inhale your power.

The breath is the energy of manifestation, of the realisation of your thought.

By inhaling you call on the divine energy within you.

※

Clarity.

Before any desire can create, your heart and your spirit must be clear. Confusion drains your energy and furthermore carries itself into the manifestation of your desires.

Like a sky without clouds – spirit clarified, the heart in peace –
thought will be able to germinate inside you like a seed.

Concentrate in order to define it clearly, forget nothing.

Be sure that you know your thought, that you desire it, for it is
what will appear before you.

Now love it. It will grow inside you, it will need love to develop
harmoniously. Love is the essential climate to exalt beauty and joy.

Visualise this seed in a sky of serene virgin love, which dwells in
you.

Then decide to make it grow in you.
Wrap it with your breath.
Send it your purest breath.
Watch it grow.
It will surround you, fill you.

Thus, this seed will become another ethereal body.
Visualise its growth.

Now set it free.
Let it go toward its manifestation, send it love and be confident.

Let this thought fly away.

It will detach itself from you and manifest in the universe.
Once manifested, it will come back to encounter you.

Purity of heart
Clarity of spirit
Desire
Will, intent

Love
Breath
Freedom
Confidence
.

.

.

Manifestation

Creation

Finally, I feel ready to work with the Spirit again in order to advance the world.

∞

I believe that creation is a back-and-forth movement.

We must take care of ourselves before we can help advance the world.

The first link in the chain, so to speak.

Each person is a first link.

Each person has the sublime power within to raise his own light and later give it to others.

∞

Enlighten yourself to enlighten the world.

∞

Creation passes through an internal pathway; first the discovery of self, then the will to return to truth and purity, then harmonious union with the cosmos.

∞

At this point a being becomes a perfect instrument of creation.

∞

An instrument for receiving energy, 'inspiration', then an instrument for manifestation, 'the gift'.

Creation in Harmony with God

I would like to explain our work on earth.

Essentially, we have a divine power of creation, it is an etheric endeavour.

◌

It is a work of creation at the level of thought and of energies, which pass through:

- ~ the heart's desire, a spontaneous source of joy, followed by
- ~ defining its manifestation as precisely as possible, then by
- ~ directing etheric energies toward the project: interior energies, celestial energies (prayer, sharing the project with Heaven), then by
- ~ confidence in heaven, listening for signals, then by
- ~ setting the scene or seizing the opportunity.

◌

For we incarnated beings, this approach to creation is a way to connect divine power to matter and to become God's instrument in the realisation of projects.

◌

This method demands iron discipline, and this creation will realise itself:

- ~ if your desire is absolutely pure and unegoistical, coming solely from the heart,
- ~ if we evolve towards the growth of divine consciousness and a purification of our beings,
- ~ if we always give God His place inside us, through meditations and prayers . . .

237

This phase of etheric creation opens up to beings who have practised the purification of their mental, emotional and physical bodies on the one hand, and on the other, expressed the wish to work with God and to live in His divine stream.

This method of creation is a round trip between heaven and earth.

Desire is sent out, energies are held in place, manifestation begins for the first time; imprecisely and remotely, or simply through the confirming signs.

In this way desire confronts the first manifestation and refines itself with reference to the first results.

Desire refines itself, becomes more precise and develops.

God will then give His advice through the heart.

Then heaven will again deploy energies that are surely imperceptible to the human eye.

The project goes back to reform itself in heaven before manifesting on earth for the second time.

It is a process of coming and going, which must occur in total confidence; always in meditation, in purity, and, above all, in the spirit of letting go.

When the project manifests itself partially or incorrectly, human beings may seize it and model it themselves with their terrestrial means.

That can break the chain, the fluidity of the action between Heaven and Earth.

We must stay steadfastly connected to our hearts and to the truth of desire, *totally*.

Never ignore the signs from the heart, even though they seem outlandish or difficult to understand, for they are fundamental to the outcome of the project.

The Channel of God

To grow to be a channel of God
   requires a pure, sacred balance,
   it is absolutely unique, it is absolute,
   it is divine, it is ecstatic,
   it is marvellous, it is delicate.

෪

To place oneself at this magical point of the universe is to offer God an extremely pure channel, one without parasites, for his arrival on earth.

෪

To place yourself in the purity of this receptacle of God is to offer yourself a few seconds or a few hours of divinity.

෪

It is a divine ecstasy.

෪

You have laboured to be pure.
   Then God comes into you.
   Then He is content, you are content,
   He is joyous, you are joyful.
   You, He and you, look at the world with your eyes of infinite love.
   You, you and He, will blow the pure energy of love into the world.
   You, you and He, will think beautiful thoughts of love for the world; and the world recreates itself before you, thanks to you, Him and you, you remember.
   The recreated world will return the flow of energy to you, you and Him.

෪

You are the channel; you have had it within yourself since birth. From the day of your birth, your soul has been calling to you, asking you to rediscover it, to purify it in order to receive God.

❦

Your soul belongs to God.

It is your ambassador at His side.

It is you beside Him in permanence.

When it speaks to you, listen; what it tells you is surely divine.

Hear its motherly counsels.

It wishes everything wonderful for you.

❦

Recover the purity of the channel; it is marvellous.

For a few moments you become God,

you are a receptacle of love,

you can give to others,

you can create beauty,

you are divine, you are finally happy, in accord with your soul and with your Father, the Creator.

The Memory of the Soul

Suspended in the cosmos . . . Am I about to detach myself from these terrestrial ties, the bonds of personality?

❧

Yes, in some way. It is difficult for a human to experience the renunciation of these attachments that rivet us to the world of mankind. Thanks to them, you are well propped up, fenced, encircled, 'loved' or 'not loved'; in any case, you have your landmarks.

❧

Yes, I find myself without landmarks.

No real family, no religion, no society, no social game . . .

❧

Nothing can really cling to me, or I to it, owing to my lucidity and especially my existential impossibility.

In fact, from the moment I participate in an illusion, or a human game, I empty myself, I suffer immediately, it is awful.

So I must renounce it at once or let myself be suffocated.

❧

It is a sensation of drifting between two worlds, detached but still afraid.

❧

I drift and I am afraid.

I am afraid of no longer being surrounded by my love, for I know that love leads me back to something 'concrete'; the realisation of myself.

I feel a terrible anxiety at this emptiness.

❧

In moments of intense peace, when the city is asleep or nearly dead, this anxiety builds. I feel emptiness becoming immense.

Fear overtakes me.

This void scares me.

Everything collapses around me. I no longer feel these attachments. There is nothing to hold me back either.

I am gripped with a longing not to live like this any longer.

It is uncomfortable. I no longer belong to anything or anyone. I am a nothing. I feel my substance slipping away.

୨୧

I understand.

I engaged to unveil the world's lie, to detach myself from it so that I could refind my truth.

Now, when I find myself again in this emptiness, in this calm, I get frightened, I cannot find myself. I have the impression that there is nothing left, no one left any more.

୨୧

Where is my essence, where am I?

In this panic I forget who I am.

୨୧

I have not come to play the game and leave again.

I am not an ego.

I am a soul.

A soul incarnated into a human body.

୨୧

I came for something else.

I came to create, to repair, to give out light.

I came in the service of God.

୨୧

At this point, my soul panics.

୨୧

The game is unveiled, the game is finished.

My soul panics because it fails to pass on to the next level of its own realisation.

243

It fears not to be able, not to know how to live outside this game, so it panics.

℘

This sensation of being without attachments is obviously an illusion, for in such moments I lose the sense of who I am, where I come from . . .

In my panic I reduce myself to the personality that attempts to play but which has been so significantly diminished by my labours of purification, that it has no longer a reason to be or to attach.

I reduced myself to something minimal. This something can no longer tie itself to the world, it has become totally insignificant. How desperate to surprise oneself in such a mistake!

℘

I am me and I forget, or maybe I am afraid to become me.

I am me and I put myself outside of me!

℘

True, when I participate in the game, sometimes I leave my etheric body and live my incarnated life more intensely, through illusion.

Then I lose the thread, I identify with humans, with their game . . .

And there my foot slips and my soul panics.

℘

The crisis of anxiety stems from the loss of memory of who I am, of why I came . . .

My soul is suffering from loss of memory.

It cannot bear it and then it manifests before me during these terrible moments.

℘

To retrieve memory and honour the soul.

The Anguish of the Soul

After a week of agitation, during the first minutes of this greatly needed rest, anguish springs suddenly from my heart, from my body, and sweat invades the palms of my hands and the soles of my feet.

❧

No reason, no explanation.

❧

Just a thundering within myself. A fearsome vertigo. Strong and furtive. Powerful and fast. Invading, but imperceptible.

❧

Nothing tells me where it comes from. Nothing will come to help me. A violent anxiety. Against myself. Am I mad? Who is trying to make me crazy? Who is trying to make me believe in madness?

❧

Here it is, a powerful spiritual path, a wisdom gathered with all my strength and reached in agitation.

❧

The abyss.
   The abyss of human madness. Even if it only lasts a few seconds. Some miasma of life come to blacken the picture, spoiling life, rotting the fruit that was so wonderfully cultivated in this new Garden of Eden.

❧

We try to free ourselves from it as if it were an untimely spider. We throw it into the nettles.

❧

We return to ourselves.

We find joy again.

Then life starts to flow again without us having to think about it too much, but always in the secret hope of understanding.

Understanding who plays the devil in this dark corner of myself.

A place I never reached into deeply enough to dislodge the non-love, the non-light, the fear, the illusion made law.

∞

Surreptitiously, an idea murmurs in my ear, a thought from far away.

∞

The anguish of the void.

∞

This classic fear would come back to see me, after I had done so much work on myself, after all my discoveries about myself and humanity, after such a powerful desire for union with God, after, after, after . . .

∞

A spiritual road that was so powerful, so remarkable, of such rejoicing that I could never have imagined returning to this primal fear of human beings.

∞

The fear of emptiness has indeed come back to scorn me with its violent emotional pickaxes, its existential threats.

∞

What misery to see it again, to see it resurface in me!

It is another level, they will tell me.

∞

You would say it is interesting – but what suffering, what disappointment!

From now on my soul will bring out all the accumulated sorrow on this earth.

∞

The anguish of the void.

We felt it at the outset of the spiritual path.

It is what has steered us, using its power, using its torture, towards understanding the meaning of life, towards seeking out the answer.

That is what put me back on the road of truth.

That is what led me to re-encounter my celestial companions, my essence, my presence near God and God Himself.

∞

Yes, but suffering in ignorance is terrible.

The unknown is vast.

The anguish of emptiness leads us to infinitesimal finiteness, to smallness in the face of the ferocious and uncontrollable immensity of the world.

∞

Bounced about in the infinite. No landmarks. No protection. Leading into nothingness. No lifelines . . .

My soul was about to make things known to me.

I had already lived through it with my personality at the beginning of my path to truth.

Here I am face to face with my soul, relieved of the majority of my personality's masks.

∞

My soul comes to deliver up its secrets.

∞

Yes, my soul also suffers anxieties, fears and flaws that must be cleansed.

It is now time to take the path that will lead us to the purification of the soul.

It is a grand stage which will lead us to our divine presence and our mission.

Embrace Your Shadow

An extremely profound silence.

Nothing. No whispering, no rustling.

Simply a notion of emptiness, which surrounds me slowly and surreptitiously.

❧

I was not aware until the moment anxiety surfaced to squeeze my throat. Why this anguish?

❧

The silence frightened me.

I felt the fear. Fear of not being supported by anything, of simply floating in space.

❧

Yes, it is true, sometimes this state of grace, outside of time and space, terrifies me.

I cannot perceive matter around me; I don't feel tied to anything here; nothing clings to me any more. What will I become?

❧

In these moments of disconnection from the world of matter, something inside me starts to frighten me; it plays with me.

❧

This is my ego, it does not want to allow me to fly off to the land of the angels where it certainly has no place, where it will certainly disintegrate because its energy is too low.

❧

At the precise moment when my ears cease to give me the sound of the world, when my senses no longer capture the matter that surrounds me, my ego resurges, knowing that I am preparing to 'take off', to leave three-dimensional reality for a moment.

At this instant my spirit joins my soul again, and my being vibrates at a new level of different energy; little by little I fuse with the etheric world.

Beyond that, it cannot follow me; its energy is too low.

Beyond that, it has nothing to hang on to; its attempts to seize the power are vain, invisible, nil.

❧

So at the point where peace dwells in me; where my spirit escapes the social, mental, material and emotional tumult; when the energy of my being rises up, my ego panics.

It feels attacked, abandoned. It fears for its existence and there it begins to play the subtle game of fear.

It will analyse the weaknesses of my being, my spirit, my aura.

❧

Where do doubt, fear, separation, illusion, and non-light still lodge? Where do the low energies still dissimulate?

❧

The more the spirit reaches elevated spheres of purity and energy, the less numerous and visible is the zone of shadow and of low energy.

The more the spirit purifies itself, the subtler the game of the ego becomes in order to prevent its extinction or, rather, its transmutation.

❧

Thus the ego revives all the old wolves and activates them in such moments of peace and spiritual progression.

❧

At the start of the spiritual path, it will draw you into traps relating to personality; these are the 'first layers' of non-loving behaviour.

Then, it will progressively flush out all repressed behaviours one after another.

❧

In fact, throughout our lives, each one of us has concealed certain tendencies, wants and gifts due to worry over social integration, due to our desire to be loved and accepted . . .

oջ

It was shameful to have felt aggressiveness, or the desire to abandon everything or to become an outsider.

Thus, each of us needed to conceal the refusal of self, of desires, of spontaneity, and of our gifts early on; to bury them deep inside ourselves until we forgot them.

oջ

That is how the forgotten places of memory and of life reside in each of us.

oջ

But in reality these refusals still live in us, in the shadow.

They await the return of the Light, liberation, release of truth.

They await recognition as your own children, as part of yourself.

In actuality, they are the parts of you which you have left behind on the road.

oջ

Today you are living without them, you have forgotten them.

In reality, you are incomplete without them.

Meanwhile, they exist in a cave within you.

In your desire to find truth on the spiritual path, they will reappear, one after the other, without exception.

oջ

It is true that discovery is sometimes painful, or at any rate charged with emotion.

When you have to disown part of yourself, it is realised in the suffering, in the emotional shock of denying self and of refusing truth and thus love.

Thus, it is through pain and emotional shock that this ancient, forgotten part of yourself will resurface.

oջ

Spiritual evolution consists of finding these pieces of yourself again, with understanding and compassion for the being that you were, who suffered from fragility and shame.

∾

You are being led to recover your memory, as one recalls a far-away dream.

This will initiate an emotional jolt of your memory.

It is a buried emotion that covers up a hidden reality.

∾

You have suffered from being unable to express your truth, however good or bad.

You were ashamed to expose your reality: for example, the wish to scream or to sing; or a desire for aggression or for loving . . .

You were ashamed to live on the fringes, to be dismissed to your solitude, to be ridiculous . . .

You simply said 'no' to your spontaneity; you did not betray anything, you never voiced your feelings.

You imposed internal suffering upon yourself rather than baring your soul.

∾

This is the emotion through which your memory will resurface.

∾

Memory recollects itself just as a dream resurges, by analogy of situation, of objects, of people, of tastes, of smells, of noises, of facts, of emotions . . .

∾

The ego, which you patiently try to take care of all along your spiritual path, will play the game of fear with these buried memories.

∾

Instead of reconciling you to these hidden fractions of yourself, it will try to separate you from them.

It will try to emphasise the space which separates you from your parts.

251

It will insert fear between you and them, that is to say, between you and you.

It will attempt to create separation in your innermost self.

How?

The ego reactivates the parts that you have repulsed from shame.

It will encourage you to repel them once more by integrating your fear of seeing them reappear.

So it makes you believe that they do not belong to you and moreover, that you have to fight them, chase them off lest they lead you back into shame and failure.

❧

Using these methods, it will try to scare you regarding the parts you had already repressed.

True enough, the more one represses something, the more forcefully it clings.

It is a vicious circle.

Your ego tries to convince you of the need for separation: these parts are harmful and must be driven out.

Now you are afraid when memory resurges.

Then you attempt to chase this memory away.

You want to rid yourself of it.

Of course, it resurges more violently, for it is part of you, it is your history, it is yourself.

So then you get more intensely frightened and try to chase it off again, and so it goes on.

This is how you are trapped into fear of these repressed remembrances.

You are afraid of what is inside you.

So your ego has the upper hand.

You still need it.

You are still living in fear.

❧

The inverse mechanism is that of recognising ourselves and our repressions, which are really indications of our interior riches.

❧

We must pull out of the fear of seeing inner ghosts wandering about, open our eyes, kindle the light, go through the lost emotions, and see.

❧

See what did not have the keys to the city.

See and understand this child that tried to survive in the world of judgments and codes.

This child did indeed feel the desire to break everything in order to express himself.

It was legitimate violence.

It has to be known, understood, excused and loved.

To love this child and understand that behind the violence hid the delicate flower of the gift, of the beauty.

This is a vexed child.

How can you fear him? How can you not turn to him?

❧

You must give him his right to speak.

You must allow him to dry his tears, to quieten his anger.

You must give him love.

Only then can he heal and give himself to you again.

Only then will your hidden, repressed parts come forth.

Only then will you be whole, and in peace.

❧

Do not forget, however, to love this ego that caused you to know the world and which, through its fear, led you back to the cognition of your self.

Look after it so it cannot take you back into fear.

Take care of it, so that it will be able to rediscover your divinity.

253

The Opening of Consciousness

Beloved, in these last few days your being has been shaken.
  You experienced self-doubt.
  Thus, you have narrowed the field of your consciousness.

❧

Yes, God is infinite consciousness.
  God multiplied himself and created us.
  You are God. You are infinite.

❧

Everything is part of universal consciousness.
  Everything is a function of it.
  Reducing it or expanding it is all that each one of us does at each moment of his existence, with each breath. Each one of us decides to experience a fuller or a narrower consciousness. Each action leads you to one or the other.

❧

When you decide to rediscover your soul, you set out to rejoin your true divine nature, of infinite consciousness.

❧

The infinite consciousness is God.

❧

God is infinite. You are part of it. You are this unlimited consciousness. You are, within you, what God is. This totality, this unity of being is in you. It is incredible but that is at the heart of your heart.

❧

It is a point where you come to fuse totally with this infinity.
  This point is inside you.

You alone can find it, alone in your plenitude and your serenity, alone in the profound desire to find it again.

༄

This point is the portal of the universe, toward infinity.

༄

It is the exact place where each sage attempts to lead his spirit, his consciousness, knowing it to be the point of departure for the infinite.

༄

Doubt is a sentiment that removes you from this place, keeps you distant from it. It is then that you feel lost, reduced to a limited consciousness. You have lost the track to this magic environment. You have then lost even the memory of it. So you reduce your consciousness to the fears that doubt will resurface in us. In this confusion you must remember again, must try to recapture confidence, rediscover the place.

༄

How to attain this place?

It is the anchoring point of your divinity.

It is there that your soul reduces itself to incarnate into this body.

So when you desire to find yourself again, to meditate, it is simply that you perceive the need to reconnect to your real nature, which is your divinity.

You will try to cleanse yourself, to find peace within because you know that something awaits you there, at this precise point.

This place is your centre.

We often call it the heart centre.

It is the divinity of your being, which has fused there.

You will be authorised to go there when you are on the quest for your purity, when you bathe in an elevated energy.

༄

It is then that you will be able to live the true value of your being, your real spiritual power, your immense gifts and, surely, your divine liberty.

Dialogue of Our Souls

It is not the words that we have exchanged together; it is not the ideas or the so-called discoveries that we have formulated together that moved me.

❧

Words to cover what passed from you to me, from me to you.
  Words without importance but words like shy petticoats.

❧

Yes, it was a delicate beauty, a faultless beauty, a shadowless beauty, a beauty as obvious as the breath of youth, a new beauty like the blossoming of a rose, an old beauty that is found again after thousands of moments, a wise beauty, a beauty which does not see itself but simply is.

❧

Words, but above all a breath, the breath of eternal love, the divine breath of love, the breath of God. We were close, we were face to face, we were almost one.

❧

Our souls have taken the oath but our personalities remained silent.

❧

Words hummed without a true message to reassure our sleeping personalities, as one chants a lullaby to a child who refuses to abandon his toys to go to bed.

❧

During this moment, magic surrounded us.

❧

We were bathed in a light as gentle as the first night of our spiritual encounter. A gentle light as sweet as celestial love can be.

With our souls, we both went to the land of wonders; we left illusions behind for a few moments, a few instants of eternity.

I heard you.

I received messages.

I recognised the love that certain sages diffuse with their eyes, through their words, from their beings.

I recognised this energy that we receive when we are close to our souls.

I recognised it.

Your soul was speaking to me.

I could find no answer, only tell it words of love and humility.

I felt a profound shiver.

A halo of well-being.

A fear of seeing the unknown.

I felt the infinite.

The doors of my heart opened.

Opened for eternity. Opened to the infinite.

Thus I received your treasures, your wisdom and your love.

I received all of that from you; I received all of that from God.

I received them without fear because your voice is familiar to me.

The sound of your voice was familiar but the message was new.

The words were familiar but the energy was unique.

Your words were your own but they belonged to celestial love.

It is by grace of your purity and your wisdom that love can manifest itself through your being, your body, your breath and your words.

You lived in perfect harmony with your soul.

You let the divine river flood your words, your breath and your energy.

❧

Know that an exceptional being came to me in my thought the moment I felt the immensity of your message.

Know that this being was present through you.

Is it I who tells you this, is it a celestial being, who knows?

❧

To feel.

To honour the sentiments, the sensations.

To let the divine flow invade each moment of our existence.

To find our divine soul once more.

To find our ancient sages once again.

To merge our souls.

To listen.

To stay humble.

To love. To love living. To live in the divine river.

To accept our divine nature.

To listen to our desires.

To acknowledge the divine energy.

To honour. To live God. To live love. To live with love. To live for love.

❧

We have come to study the human world in order to assist them to live the love they are made of.

We came thousands of times just for that.

We were sent by our sages. They are watching us. They protect us. They send us love messages unceasingly.

❧

We shall leave when love has conquered the hearts of humans, when humanity returns to God.

Giving Birth

Thank you, God, for offering me this great gift and privilege of giving birth.

⅔

I received the gift of birthing and the gift of receiving in our midst and a marvellous being through my womb.

I know that he is divine and I do everything to maintain him in this state of divinity.

I try from my utmost to give him an ideal environment, that is to say, a universe of love, at the maximum of my actual capacity.

A universe where he shall have no fear of expressing his reality or his essence.

I don't want him to see fear loitering around him, not even a suggestion of it.

Yes, I want this child to be able to express freely what he is, what he wishes to express, and why he has come to be among us.

⅔

Knowing that this world has deviated toward fear and has revolved around fear ever since and thus around competition and struggle tests parents. And then to receive a child of God!

⅔

You know that God has sent you a pure being – marvellous, totally divine.

You know that he has come to do something divine on earth.

But you know too that this world is not in harmony with heaven or with God.

You know that love does not reign here. You know that the beings on this planet fight to survive, one against the other, and thus have lost the trace of their divinity, of their unconditional love . . .

259

❧

You receive this angel, this God.

You are overcome with joy. You are transfixed by the extraordinary, by God who is nearby.

You live the ecstasy of creation.

You nourish yourself with this sublime, pure, sweet, white, divine energy that this being carries in itself. Once more you partake of the divine.

❧

At this moment in your life, God gives you the opportunity to feel divine love.

You procreate and God gives you a new opportunity to feel His energy, the energy of angels, the energy that you yourself had at birth.

He gives you another taste of eternity.

He gives humans another choice in life.

The chance to taste unconditional love again, without limits or judgment . . .

❧

At this moment of your life, you hold the immense privilege of recovering the memory of the divine love within you, which you have denied since your tender infancy when the world made you afraid, when it judged you.

❧

You give birth and you retrieve these universal feelings of sacredness, of tenderness, of joy, of infinite love.

❧

To give birth is to offer God a welcome for one of His own.

To give birth is to become a channel between heaven and earth.

To give birth is to give your generosity to God, it is the remembrance of one's best qualities.

To give birth is to prove that God exists, that God, above all, exists in us.

To give birth is to cease to play in the egotism of the world.

To give birth is to tear up what has come to stifle our hearts; it is to open your heart wide.

❧

At this moment you can seize your chance.

The second chance to remember. Without effort.

To remember who we are.

To stop lying.

To stop struggling against the illusion of fear.

You have the opportunity to refind the road to love and truth. Make use of it then!

❧

This being, like you, came to take the pleasures of our planet; this being, like you, came to express his divinity and gifts on Earth.

Why inflict on him all the tests of non-love with which the world received you?

Why make him believe in fear?

Why drag him into the world's illusion?

Why push him into creating for himself a personality conforming to world desiderata?

Why judge him, why show him the track of lying?

Why make him believe in the need to fight for survival?

❧

No, stop this lie.

Do not be afraid; go back to your purity, your truth, to the love in you.

Find God in yourself again and speak to the new being of love.

Tell him that you love him infinitely, that you love him without limits, without conditions, without expectations.

Tell him that he is your son and the son of God.

Do not hesitate to tell him that you know he has come to offer God to you again, that while he is all love the world has forgotten it.

Explain to him that mankind has lost truth and harmony.

Tell him that humanity will judge him, will demand him to function according to its criteria.

※

But above all, tell him to refrain from playing this comedy, to remain himself, as beautiful and pure as he arrived on Earth.

Tell him to listen only to his heart, not even to your own demands.

Tell him to follow his heart's desires, to grow up in a merging with his heart, to create with his heart.

Tell him to cultivate joy, to live for nothing but joy.

One day this child will create freely, he will create in unison with God.

※

You gave yourself to God to receive one of His children, so honour him who came, honour his purity, honour his joy, honour his innocence.

Do not taint him with your lies or the ones that terrify you.

Honour his coming, honour his energy and his love, honour his nature and his desires and let him become God on Earth.

※

Seize your chance and let this child guide you toward the light, which he carries in himself, which he brought to give to the world that is so much in need of it.

※

God has come to you, honour Him.

God gave you a being of love, honour him.

God sent you an angel to bring light to the humans, help him, let him make himself happy, let him become the messenger of God on Earth.

His mission is your own.

Do not allow yourself to go along with the lies of the world.

Your mission has been to receive him.

Your mission is also to give him the freedom to be himself, to create with his soul.

※

God is generous, celebrate Him.

Reconciliation with Your Soul

Now the time has come to take care of my soul, relieve it of the pain and hurt caused by abandonment and rejection.

❧

Yes, when we adhere to the human world and decide to play the game, we create a personality and at precisely this moment we declare our abandonment.

❧

We decide to forsake our souls.

The material world proposes a program, a stake that we accept. It is a choice.

❧

To play the game of the world of the ego or to stay in the truth.

To play a new role, to construct, to create from scratch, to imagine, to elaborate, to refine . . .

❧

It is a skilful game which will in fact present many challenges to overcome, as well as new pleasures and different energies.

❧

Thus in order to play, one must forget one's real identity, one's real divine nature.

❧

To forget the soul. To reject it.

❧

This is a permanent battle.

When a being chooses to play the human game, to create an ego, to live through this new persona, the soul comes to manifest itself, to reclaim truth, to shout for help.

It will fight this superficial creation that produces very low energies.

∽

It is a battle between light and non-light.

∽

But the human world has created an illusion that is so omni-present, so powerful that beings living there will lose the force and the lucidity to remain in the light, in their truth.

∽

It is an unequal battle, certainly, but it is a battle of truth.

∽

In general, man will abandon it rapidly.

The battle terminates there when he decides to reject his soul, its messages and its cries.

First he will reject it, then he will simply forget it.

∽

To forget the soul.

∽

The human world will become his unique universe, one that is too overwhelming, where multiple and incessant challenges occupy his existence.

∽

His anger, the sorrow of his soul, will regularly seek him out.

They are perches, chances to abandon illusion.

But man no longer believes in that.

The angers and pains of his soul, manifested as 'astonishing' and 'inexplicable' events, will be attributed to nothing more than lucky or unlucky chances . . .

∽

The soul is relegated to its home turf, that of God, that of the angels.

It is now merely a spectator.

It has been rejected, along with its light, its goodness, its beauty, its love, its messages, its joy . . .

264

❧

Rejected as it was in previous lives.

No one in the land of the ego is interested in it.

❧

Its etheric power of creation, of communication, of communion with God is no longer of interest, so it will be totally lost and forgotten, pushed into the ranks of romantic, imaginary magic.

❧

The soul is alone from now on.

It suffers. It weeps. It is no longer tied to its being.

❧

Today the time has come for me to go back to the search for the soul, to console it and love it, to tell it that I can no longer live without it, without its light, without my truth, without our truth.

❧

I need it now.

❧

I took a difficult path to return to truth and light.

Along the way, I have unmasked many of my illusory creations: my personality, my false I, my attitudes, my reflexes, my fears, my egoistic desires. A whole world of illusions.

With illusions, I nourished myself.

❧

I stopped everything.

I wanted to light the torch, to let the ghosts slip away.

I have suffered with the unknown, with the terror of the void, but I knew that I was on the right road.

❧

Nothing could halt me, neither my fears nor the world's threats.

❧

Then I understood the construction of this edifice in my life. Little by little, I have dismantled it.

❧

Today, in this new virginity, in this glade that I have finally found again, I see my suffering soul.

❧

There, I abandoned and rejected it; there I have re-encountered it.

❧

I must heal it, take care of these wounds that I inflicted on it all my life long.

❧

My deepest desire to find it once more is realised.

Now is the hour to make peace, to reunite as at the moment of creation.

❧

Today I know where the truth of my heart is, I recognise the divine flow, and I recognise the low energies.

I have recovered lucidity, the capacity to become divine again.

My desire to fuse with my soul is possible anew.

I will listen to it through my heart. I will live in harmony with it, with myself.

It and me, we are one and the same when I am pure again.

❧

Nothing can stop this union, this reunion.

All obstacles and rejections become unbearable to my body, to my entire being.

My choice is more powerful than these incidental setbacks.

❧

It is true, I clutch it once more.

❧

It is a voluptuous, white immensity that opens its arms to me, then takes me in its arms, and holds me sensually until it merges with me, in me.

❧

I am reunited. My pen speaks for both of us now.

❧

This healing will take in a return to those places where I abandoned it each time and again, where I have abandoned innocence, spontaneity, purity for reasoning, decision, reflection, deviation, envy, impurity . . .

❧

Where I abandoned myself to be something else.

But why?

In order to be someone else, because being myself no longer pleased me.

But why?

If I held on to what I was, I no longer received what I desired.

Fear of not being loved any more, uncertainty.

❧

It was the uncertainty of love that led me into the fear of no longer being able to bathe in love's energy, as I did in heaven.

I believed in the dictatorship of fear.

So I listened to the consciousness of the world, which dictated a new path for me, a new way of walking, of living, of being . . .

❧

An attitude. A borrowed way to be. All a code.

A code to decode . . .

A code where you count, where you frame, where you calculate, where you distribute laurels with calculation. Living in a fenced-in world, walled-in.

❧

Walls: the soul could not follow me there.

❧

It had to let me act alone. And I was too obsessed with the prize of love energy amidst my dear humans; I did not want to give up this dream, this illusion, this mirage . . . no sooner discovered than it faded into the chaos of the world.

Disillusioned, I set out to search for truth.

To travel the path backwards. Hansel and Gretel. Stone after stone, retracing it to understand the construction of illusion inside me, so that I could better undo it. Dismantle it.

❧

To find the road of return again.

This willingness will awaken the soul, which has been asleep in its tears.

It will guide each step, and the light will grow stronger and stronger.

Night will never again fall over the forest.

❧

All the celestial beings hear the joy of your soul and thus participate in your journey.

At the end of your journey there is a glade where your soul awaits for you.

It is here that you will at last retrieve virginity at last.

It is here that you must take your time to dry the tears of your long rejected soul.

It is not time to desert.

❧

Yes, at the end of the road, it is there that everything begins or begins again.

Roll up your sleeves and construct your universe.

The one which you were promised at birth.

A universe of love, of creation, of gifts, of working with heaven . . .

❧

Before that, dry the tears of your separation one by one.

❧

I separated from myself to make myself loved by others, for I could no longer see unconditional love around me.

I did not believe that to find it I had only to look within, in my heart, to be in communion with my divine soul.

So I ran after these pieces of love that were offered me outside of myself. I altered my being.

I compromised my essence. I transformed my truth. According to someone or other.

Each person presented himself to me as a proposal of conditional love. Each one demanded to be seduced in order to love.

I responded despite my soul's refusal.

On each encounter with other people, I transformed a bit of myself to assure myself first of their interest, then of their love.

Thus I drew nourishment collected from right and left and not from the celestial energy which my soul could give me.

So I entered into the social spiral where we give only to receive, where we exist only if the other person so desires.

Each encounter became a contract to fulfil, overshadowed with the fear of failure; seduction demands a display of superficial qualities or conditions. Each encounter necessitated a usage of energies which were not available to my profound being.

Thus I emptied myself a little more every time, expecting to fill myself with the promise of love.

I emptied myself of my substance.

I received nothing but conditional love, a feeble energy.

My being nourished itself with emotional, mental and physical energies drawn from the participants of the world of the ego.

My soul was in retreat.

I was emptying myself of celestial energy.

Out of ignorance I had become bulimic in relations and challenges. Evidently, this pushed me into unbelievable fatigue, into a strong disgust with life.

On the one hand, I multiplied my attempts at seduction and brought forth enormous energies to give the other person what he desired, which was not in me. On the other hand, I received very thin satisfaction from those others, which is to say, I was loved with conditions.

But yes, my being emptied itself.

More energy. I could not survive on these ridiculous offerings of love in small packets.

I felt death near me very violently, and for no reasonable reason. The death of my energies.

My soul no longer wanted to feed me, because I was getting hysterical, moving further from my truth.

My soul belongs to God, it is God, it gives God.

God does not give Himself to illusion.

Why see death in front of me when life is flowing through my body, when my being seems absolutely in harmony with the world? No illness. No failure.

Nothing explained the presence of death in my universe, especially not so suddenly.

And so, severed from my celestial energy, disgusted by my social bulimia, I have known the throes of life dispossessed of life, of joy, of energy . . .

Then I held off everything to breathe again, to live without fetters, without expectations.

I stopped the scenario of society. I cut the circuit.

   I gathered myself together and I searched.

Here I am in the glade, together with my soul. I see again all the moments when I abandoned it.

   I can see again, slowly. It blurs.

   Surely, it all began with the quest for love around the ones who put us into the world, our parents, then, like ripples in the water, the circle widened. Family, school, work, friends, our loves . . .

The list is long but the reunions are beautiful.

   To weep with joy.

   To laugh with grief.

I know this is a second birth.